D1527542

New Songs of Inspiration

VOLUME TEN

Formerly distributed by
The Benson Company
Compiled by W. ELMO MERCER

Home Edition (Sturdy paper)	BS426
Church Edition (Limp)	BS427
Cloth Edition	BS428

STAMPS-BAXTER MUSIC
OF THE ZONDERVAN CORPORATION
P O BOX 4007 | DALLAS, TEXAS 75208 | 214 943-1155

6-83

"Your Gospel Music People"

FOREWORD

It is the opinion of many that in our day, more than ever before, we need a song to sing. A meaningful, scriptural, uplifting song of hope for this troubled generation. A song which tells anew the story of Jesus — his birth, his life, his death, his resurrection, his second coming, his love, his promises — sung by children of God in praise to the King of kings.

Lift high your song! Let it help unite us, regardless of our varied backgrounds and differences, in service and in love.

ACKNOWLEDGEMENTS

The Inspiration series has traditionally contained the great old songs and hymns of the revered writers of the past. From the rich legacy of praise and worship of these devout hearts we have chosen many of the songs for this collection.

Men and women like W. H. Doane, Fanny J. Crosby, Howard E. Smith, J. Edwin McConnell, George Bernard, B. B. McKinney, N. B. Vandall, P. P. Bliss, James D. Walbert, W. B. Walbert, Harry Dixon Loes, Robert Lowry, A. H. Ackley, C. C. Stafford, G. T. Speer, Will M. Ramsey, J. H. Fillmore, E. M. Bartlett, William Edie Marks, Luther G. Presley, Adger M. Pace, R. E. Winsett, Emmett S. Dean, Charles D. Tillman, J. B. Coates, Hamp Sewell, Charles Gabriel, Charles P. Jones, G. C. Morris, F. M. Lehman, George C. Stebbins, Johnson Oatman, Jr., Charles Weigle, Brantley George, James Rowe, V. O. Stamps, Charles Durham, Thomas Ramsey, A. J. Showalter, C. Austin Miles, Wm. M. Golden, J. M. Henson, Charles E. Moody, Thomas J. Laney, J. E. Thomas, Wm. S. Pitts.

From the songwriters and composers of today we have included a wide variety of new songs and special favorites. We are indebted to such writers as Ira Stanphill, Marvin P. Dalton, John R. Sweeney, Theodore Sisk, Albert E. Brumley, Cleavant Derricks, John W. Peterson, Ben Speer, Alphus LeFevre, Al Harkins, Lois Irwin, Dottie Rambo, Ralph Carmichael, Gordon Jensen, Steve Adams, Jim Hill, Shirley Cohron, Gil Moegerle, Walt Mills, Richard Blanchard, Del Delamont, Gloria and Bill Gaither, Phil Johnson, Jim Wood, Beth Glass, A. J. Sims, John Stallings, Henry Slaughter, Harold Lane, Dallas Holm, Wayne Hilliard, Marietta and Lanny Wolfe, Danny Lee, Dave Redman, LaVerne Tripp, Mosie Lister, Marcia and W. Elmo Mercer, V. B. (Vep) Ellis, E. W. (Bill) Suggs, Ray Overholt, Magdalene Crocker, Jack Hayford, Steve Stone, Elmer Cole, Ruth Munsey, Jack Campbell, Squire Parsons, Jr., Chuck Millhuff, Charles B. Wycuff, Charles B. Feltner, Byron L. Whitworth, Lowell Lundstrom, Dale Oldham.

DEDICATION

This new book is prayerfully dedicated to everyone involved with Gospel music — by writing, arranging, publishing, singing, recording, distributing, promoting, and listening! Our Heavenly Father is the Creator and Sustainer of these songs...to Him be praise and glory forever.

INSPIRATION

Alleluia

1

Jerry Sinclair

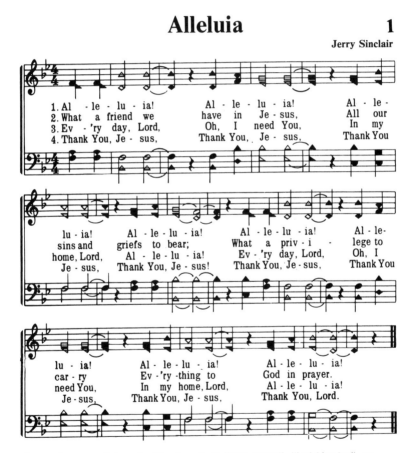

1. Al - le - lu - ia! Al - le - lu - ia! Al - le -
2. What a friend we have in Je - sus, All our
3. Ev - 'ry day, Lord, Oh, I need You, In my
4. Thank You, Je - sus, Thank You, Je - sus, Thank You

lu - ia! Al - le - lu - ia! Al - le - lu - ia! Al - le -
sins and griefs to bear; What a priv - i - lege to
home, Lord, Al - le - lu - ia! Ev - 'ry day, Lord, Oh, I
Je - sus, Thank You, Je - sus! Thank You, Je - sus, Thank You

lu - ia! Al - le - lu - ia! Al - le - lu - ia!
car - ry Ev - 'ry -thing to God in prayer.
need You, In my home, Lord, Al - le - lu - ia!
Je - sus, Thank You, Je - sus, Thank You, Lord.

You may adapt your own lyrics such as "I am Yours, Lord", "Soon returning", "Lord, I love You", etc.

2 The Year When Jesus Comes

L.W.

Lanny Wolfe

(1) What if this would be the year when Je-sus comes, _____ The year
(2) What if this would be the day when Je-sus comes, _____ The day
(3) What if this would be the mo-ment Je-sus comes, _____ The mo-

that we've been waiting for so long! _____ We'd have so lit-tle time
that we've been waiting for so long! _____ We'd have so lit-tle time
ment we've been waiting for so long! _____ We'd have no time, no time

to get our lost world won _____ If this would be the year when
to get our lost world won _____ If this would be the day when
to get our lost world won _____ If this would be the mo-ment

FINE   VERSE: (ad lib)

Je - sus comes! _____
Je - sus comes! _____   1. Years have come and years have gone since _____ Je - sus
Je - sus comes! _____   2. He   will come so quickly _____ in the twinkling

went a - way, Leav-ing us a promise that He'll come a - gain some-day, And
of   an eye, In a mo-ment we think not, He'll split the east - ern sky, And

Holy Spirit, Flow Through Me 3

W. M

Walt Mills

1. Ho - ly Spir - it, _____ _____ Flow through me; _____
2. Ho - ly Spir - it, _____ _____ Rest on me; _____
3. Ho - ly Spir - it, _____ Flow out from me; _____

Ho - ly Spir - it, _____ _____ Flow through me; _____ And
Ho - ly Spir - it, _____ _____ Rest on me; _____ And
Ho - ly Spir - it, _____ Flow out from me; _____ That

make _____ my life _____ _____ what it ought to be; _____
use _____ me Lord, _____ to win the lost to Thee; _____
oth - ers, Lord, _____ _____ may see you in me; _____

Ho - ly Spir - it, _____ Flow through me. _____
Ho - ly Spir - it, _____ Rest on me. _____
Ho - ly Spir - it, Flow out from me. _____

4

We'll Cast Our Crowns
At His Feet

G. J.

Gordon Jensen

1. When earth's short day ___ is far ___ be - hind, And heav - en's
2. We'll soon ___ for - get ___ the trou - bled path, ___ For now ___ a

role ___ com - plete; The One ___ Who saved us will say, ___ "Well
gold - en street ___ Is lead - ing us ___ to where ___ we

CHORUS:

done", We'll cast our crowns at His feet. ___ We'll cast our crowns at His
all ___ will cast our crowns at His feet. ___

nail-scarred feet, ___ Our joy complete in His presence sweet; E - ter - ni -

ty's great-est priv - 'lege will be, Cast-ing our crowns at His feet. ___

Fill My Cup, Lord

5

R. B.

Richard Blanchard

1. Like the wo-man at the well I was seeking For things that could not
2. There are mil-lions in this world who are craving The pleasure earthly
3. So, my bro-ther, if the things this world gave you Leave hungers that won't

sat - is - fy. And then I heard my Sav-ior speaking: "Draw from my
things afford. But none can match the wond'rous treasure ____ that I
pass a - way, My bless-ed Lord will come and save you ____ if you

CHORUS

well that nev-er shall run dry!"____ Fill my cup, Lord, I lift it
find in Je-sus Christ, my Lord. ____
kneel to Him and hum-bly pray: ____

up, Lord ____ Come and quench this thirsting of my soul. Bread of hea-ven,

feed me till I want no more, Fill my cup, fill it up and make me whole.

6
D. D.

King Jesus

Del Delamont

1. All the ar - mies of the world will some day gath - er, ___ And they'll
2. Un - obscured the sun will drive a - way the shad - ow, ___ At the

pass be - fore the great re - view - ing stand, And they'll beat their swords and
dawn - ing of that great e - ter - nal day, And there'll be no sounds of

wea - pons in - to plowshares, ___ And the Prince of Peace shall give the last com -
cry - ing in the ghet - tos, ___ For all grief and pain and death shall pass a -

CHORUS:

mand. ___ When King Je - sus comes to live with us a - gain, ___ He will show His
way. ___

right - eous love to ev - 'ry man, ___ Wars and strife will all be past, There'll be

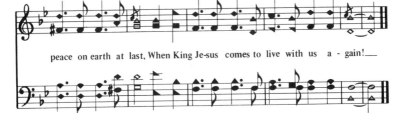

peace on earth at last, When King Je-sus comes to live with us a - gain!

I Shall Be At Home With Jesus 7

Jennie Wilson   With feeling   James D. Vaughan

1. Years of time are swift-ly pass-ing, Bring-ing near-er heaven's goal;
2. Aft - er all the days of wait-ing, For His voice to bid me come,
3. Aft - er leav-ing earth-ly pathways, Which my wea-ry feet have pressed,
4. Aft - er last farewells are spok-en, I shall meet dear ones I've known,

Soon I'll be at home with Je-sus, While e - ter - nal a - ges roll.
I shall walk be-side my Sav-iour, 'Mid bright scenes where an - gels roam.
I shall stray by life's fair riv - er, Find-ing ho - ly peace and rest.
In the presence of our Saviour, When we stand be - fore His throne.

CHORUS

O how pre-cious is the promise, That with glad-ness fills my soul!

I shall be at home with Je-sus, While e - ter - nal a - ges roll!

8
Going Home

William J. & Gloria Gaither

William J. Gaither

1. Man-y times in my child-hood when we'd trav-el so far; By
2. Now the twi-light is fad-ing and the day soon shall end; I get
3. Oh, my heart gets so hea-vy and I'm long-ing to see All my

night-fall how wea-ry I'd grow; Fa-ther's arm would slip 'round me
home-sick the far-ther I roam; But my Fa-ther has led me
loved ones and friends I have known; Ev-'ry step draws me near-er

CHORUS:

so gent-ly He'd say, "My child, we're GO-ING HOME."
each step of the way; and now we're GO-ING HOME. GO-ING
to the land of my dreams, Praise God, I'm GOING HOME. Oh, I'm

HOME, I'M GO-ING HOME There's noth-ing to
go-ing home, Yes, I'm go-ing home, No, there's

hold me here; Well, I've caught a glimpse of that
noth-ing to hold me here; Yes, I've caught a glimpse

Hea - ven - ly land, Praise God, I'm GO - ING HOME.
of that Heav'n-ly land

What A Glad Reunion Day 9

W. E. M.

W. Elmo Mercer

1. Soon my Lord will call for me, Friends and loved ones I shall see,
2. When I reach the oth - er side, What a glad re - un - ion day! Heav - en's gates will o - pen wide, What a glad re - un - ion day!
3. Then to Je - sus let me go, Where the heal - ing wa - ters flow,
4. At the feet of Christ, my Lord, We shall sing in one ac - cord,

CHORUS

Some bright morn - ing I shall fly a - way;
Yes, some bright and hap - py morn - ing

Hal - le - lu - jah, What a glad re - un - ion day.
Hal - le - lu - jah, I will shout, Oh,

10 God's Gonna Bless His Children

P. J.

Phil Johnson

God's ___ gon - na bless His chil - dren, _____

___ God's ___ gon - na care ___ for His

fam - 'ly; _____ He'll al - ways _____ have e -

nough of ev - 'ry - thing _____ we need; _____

___ God's ___ gon - na care, _____ God's

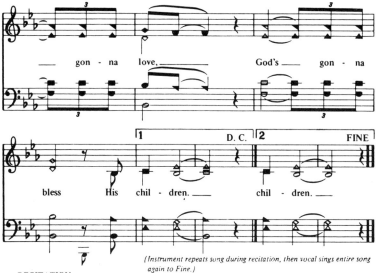

gon - na love,_____ God's _____ gon - na

bless His chil - dren. _____ chil - dren. _____

(Instrument repeats song during recitation, then vocal sings entire song again to Fine.)

RECITATION:

Although the fig tree shall not blossom, Yet I will rejoice in the Lord;
  Neither shall fruit be in the vines and the labor of the olive may fail;
    Yet I will rejoice in my Lord!
And the fields shall yeild no meat, the flock may be cut off from the fold,
  Yet I will rejoice in the Lord.
There may be no herd in the stalls, but yet I will rejoice in my Lord.
I will joy in the God of my salvation; You see, the Lord God is my strength;
And He will make my feet like hind's feet, and He shall make me to walk upon high places,
  I will rejoice in the Lord! (from Habakkuk 3:17, 19)

Give Me Jesus

11

Unknown

Arr. John Moore

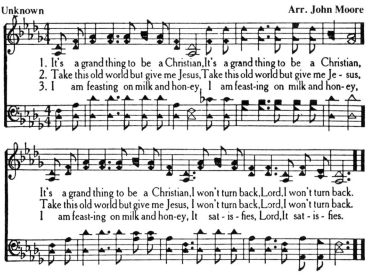

1. It's a grand thing to be a Christian, It's a grand thing to be a Christian,
2. Take this old world but give me Jesus, Take this old world but give me Je - sus,
3. I   am feasting on milk and hon-ey, I am feast-ing on milk and hon-ey,

It's a grand thing to be a Christian, I won't turn back, Lord, I won't turn back.
Take this old world but give me Jesus, I won't turn back, Lord, I won't turn back.
I   am feast-ing on milk and hon-ey, It sat - is - fies, Lord, It sat - is - fies.

12 Tears Will Never Stain the Streets
of That City

D. R.

Dottie Rambo

1. If____ I could count the tears____ that have fal - en, ____
2. I've____ nev - er met one man____ with - out sor - row, ____
3. I have ques - tioned the loss____ of a loved one, ____

____ It would seem like an o - cean to me;____ And if my
____ Nev - er looked in - to eyes with no pain;____ But there's a
____ The____ grave seems so fi - nal and cold;____ ____ But we'll

heart____ were a win - dow you could look____ through, ____ ____
land____ where____ grief____ is a____ stran - ger, ____ ____ And
meet a - gain where death____ has no____ vic - t'ry, ____ In a

CHORUS:

Oh the pain and scars____ you would see. _____ But
joy____ is the on - ly song they sing. _____ And tears____ will
land____ where we'll ne - ver grow old. _____ And

nev - er stain the streets of that ci - ty, ____ No wreaths of death on

my man-sion door;___ Tear-drops aren't welcome be-yond the gates of

glo-ry,___ 'Cause the heart will nev-er break ___ an-y-more.___

O Come, Angel Band

13

Jefferson Hascall

W. B. Bradbury

1 { My lat-est sun is sink-ing fast, My race is near-ly run,
My strong-est tri-als now are past, My tri-umph is be-gun!

2 { I know I'm near-ing ho-ly ranks Of friends and kin-dred dear;
I brush the dew of Jordan's banks, The cross-ing must be near;

3 { I've al-most gained my heav'n-ly home, My spir-it loud-ly sings;
The ho-ly ones, be-hold, they come! I hear the noise of wings,

4 { O bear my long-ing heart to Him Who bled and died for me;
Whose blood now clean-ses from all sin, And gives me vic-to-ry.

Refrain f

O come, an-gel band, come, and around me stand, O bear me a-way on your

snow-y wings To my im-mor-tal home my im-mor-tal home.

14
Here They Come

J. W. and B. G.

Jim Wood & Beth Glass

1. Ga - briel's gold - en trum - pet sounds, all the saints will leave the ground,
2. Here comes Mom and here comes Dad, oh, their fac - es look so glad,

They are ris - ing up to meet the bless - ed Lord; Oh, how they
As they march____ and they sing re - demp - tion's song; Oh, what a

shout____ as they rise to their home be - yond the skies, They're in the
smile up - on their face as they sing "A - maz - ing Grace", They're in the

CHORUS

Bride of Christ, and they are com - ing home. And here they come, ____
Bride of Christ, and they are com - ing home. Here they come,

oh, what____ a thrill! _____ Here they come, marching up to
what a thrill!

Zi - on's hill; The vic - t'ry's won as they bow be - fore

Vic-t'ry's won

God's Son, The Bride of Je - sus is com-ing home!

My Jesus, I Love Thee

15

Anonymous

A. J. Gordon

1. My Je - sus, I love Thee, I know Thou art mine, For Thee all the
2. I love Thee, be-cause Thou hast first lov - ed me, And purchased my
3. I'll love Thee in life, I will love Thee in death, And praise Thee as
4. In man-sions of glo - ry and end - less de - light, I'll ev - er a -

fol - lies of sin I re - sign; My gra-cious Re - deem - er, my Sav-
par - don on Cal-va-ry's tree; I love Thee for wear - ing the thorns
long as Thou lend-est me breath; And say when the death - dew lies cold
dore Thee in heav-en so bright; I'll sing with the glit - ter-ing crown

ior art Thou; If ev - er I loved Thee, my Je - sus, 'tis now.
on Thy brow; If ev - er I loved Thee, my Je - sus, 'tis now.
on my brow; If ev - er I loved Thee, my Je - sus, 'tis now.
on my brow; If ev - er I loved Thee, my Je - sus, 'tis now.

16 All Because Of God's Amazing Grace

S. R. A.

Stephen R. Adams

1. A - maz-ing grace! Oh, how sweet the sound That saved a poor
2. Thro' dis-ap - point-ment and dan - ger, too, Thro' la - bors and
3. Then with the ran-somed a - round God's throne We'll praise our Re -

sin - ner like me!____ Though once I was lost,_ Yet now_ I'm
sor-rows we've come!____ But God's grace has guid - ed safe - ly
deem - er and King!____ We'll tell how His mer-cy for sin did a -

found, Tho' I was blind-ed_ now_ I see!____ (1,2) And it's
through; And it will sure-ly_ lead_ us home!____ (3) "It was
tone, Thro' count-less a - ges this song_ we'll sing!____

CHORUS

all _ be-cause of God's a-maz-ing grace!____ Be-cause on Cal-v'ry's
all _ be-cause of God's a-maz-ing grace!____ Be-cause on Cal-v'ry's

moun-tain He took my place!_ And some-day, some glo-rious morn-ing I shall
moun-tain He took my place!" Oh! some-day,

see Him face to face, All be-cause of God's a-maz-ing grace!___

Have You Any Room For Jesus? 17

Arr. by W. W. B. from L. W. M.

C. C. Williams

1. Have you an-y room for Je-sus, He who bore your load of sin?
2. Room for plea-sure, room for busi-ness, But for Christ the Cru-ci-fied,
3. Have you an-y room for Je-sus, As in grace He calls a-gain?
4. Room and time now give to Je-sus, Soon will pass God's day of grace;

As He knocks and asks ad-mis-sion, Sin-ner, will you let Him in?
Not a place that He can en-ter, In the heart for which He died?
O to-day is time ac-cept-ed, To-mor-row you may call in vain.
Soon thy heart left cold and si-lent, And thy Sav-ior's pleading cease.

CHORUS

Room for Je-sus, King of glo-ry! Has-ten now His word o-bey;

Swing the heart's door wide-ly o-pen, Bid Him en-ter while you may.

18   I Found It All In Jesus

W. E. M.

W. Elmo Mercer

1. While I sought for rich-es and pleas-ures un-told, I longed for
2. All a-lone I had trav-eled the long road of life, Seek-ing for

peace in my heart; But when I came to Je-sus and gave Him con-
some-one who cared; When I found on-ly heart-ache and trou-ble and

CHORUS:

trol, He gave real joy from the start! I found it all in
strife, I prayed to God in des-pair.

Je-sus! My searching is through, all things are new; I found it

all in Je-sus, And you can find Him, too.

Someday I'll Walk On Gold

19

L.W.

Lanny Wolfe

1. I can - not boast of rich - es, __ No treas - ures do I
2. This life is al - most o - ver, __ My sto - ry's al - most

hold; __ But I have this bless - ed prom - ise: __ Some - day I'll
told; __ But I'll meet you up in Heav - en, __ Where we'll walk on

CHORUS:

walk on gold! __ I'll walk gold - en streets in that beau - ti - ful
streets of gold!

ci - ty, In that land where we'll never grow old; __ Tho' here be -

low I may be just a pau - per, Some-day I'll walk on gold! __

20 The Last Mile Of The Way

Rev. Johnson Oatman, Jr.   Wm. Edie Marks

1. If I walk in the pathway of du-ty, If I work till the
2. If for Christ I proclaim the glad sto-ry, If I seek for His
3. Here the dear-est of ties we must sev-er, Tears of sor-row are
4. And if here I have earn-est-ly striv-en, And have tried all His

close of the day; I shall see the great King in His beau-ty,
sheep gone a-stray, I am sure He will show me His glo-ry,
seen ev-'ry day; But no sick-ness, no sigh-ing for-ev-er
will to o-bey, 'Twill en-hance all the rap-ture of heav-en,

FINE   **CHORUS**

When I've gone the last mile of the way. When I've gone the last

D. S.-When I've gone the last mile of the way.

mile of the way,............ I will rest at the close of the
the last mile of the way,   at the

D. S.

day,........... .And I know there are joys that a-wait me,
close of the day,

The Unseen Hand

21

A. J. S.

A. J. Sims

1. There is an un - seen Hand to me ___ That leads thru ways ___
2. His hand has led ___ thru shadows drear ___ And while it leads ___
3. I long to see ___ my Sav-ior's face ___ And sing the sto -

I can-not see ___ While go - ing thru ___ this world of woe ___
I have no fear ___ I know 'twill lead ___ me to that home ___
ry saved by grace ___ And there up - on ___ that gold-en strand ___

CHORUS

This hand still leads ___ me as I go. ___
Where sin nor sor - rows e'er can come. ___ I'm trusting to ___ the unseen
I'll praise Him for ___ His guid-ing hand. ___

hand ___ That guides me thru ___ this wear-y land ___ And some sweet

day ___ I'll reach that strand ___ Still guid-ed by ___ the unseen hand. ___

22
I'll Fly Away

A. E. B.

Albert E. Brumley

1. Some glad morn-ing when this life is o'er, I'll fly a-
2. When the shad-ows of this life have grown,
3. Just a few more wea-ry days and then, fly a-way

way; To a home on God's ce-les-tial shore,
Like a bird from pris-on bars has flown,
fly a-way; To a land where joys shall nev-er end,

CHORUS

I'll fly a-way. I'll fly a-
fly a-way fly a-way. fly a-way

way, O glo-ry, I'll fly a-way; When I die,
fly a-way, in the morn-ing,

Hal-le-lu-jah, by and by, I'll fly a-way.
fly a-way fly a-way.

Love Lifted Me

23

James Rowe

Howard E. Smith

1. I was sink-ing deep in sin, Far from the peaceful shore, Ver-y deep-ly stained with-in, Sink-ing to rise no more; But the Mas-ter of the sea Heard my de-spair-ing cry, From the wa-ters lift-ed me. Now safe am I.

2. All my heart to Him I give, Ev-er to Him I'll cling, In His bless-ed pres-ence live, Ev-er His prais-es sing; Love so might-y and so true Mer-its my soul's best songs, Faith-ful, lov-ing serv-ice, too, To Him be-longs.

3. Souls in dan-ger, look a-bove, Je-sus complete-ly saves, He will lift you by His love Out of the an-gry waves; He's the Mas-ter of the sea, Bil-lows His will o-bey; He your Sav-iour wants to be—Be saved to-day.

CHORUS

Love lift-ed me! Love lift-ed me! e-ven me! e-ven me! When noth-ing else could help, Love lift-ed me. Love lift-ed me.

24
J. S.

Learning To Lean

John Stallings

I'm learn - ing to lean, learn - ing to lean, Learn - ing to
lean ___ on Je - sus; Find - ing more pow - er
than I'd ev - er dreamed; I'm learn - ing to lean on

Last time to

VERSE

Je - sus. ___

1. The joy I can't ex - plain ___
2. Sometimes ___ we can be ___
3. ___ Sad, ___ bro - ken heart - ed,
4. There's glo - ri - ous vic - t'ry

___ fills ___ my soul, Since ___ the day I
like the man ___ who said, My life is full now,
___ so oft - en ___ I've knelt, And ___ I've found
___ each day now ___ for me, ___ I found

26 He Looked Beyond My Fault
(And Saw My Need)

Dottie Rambo

Adapted from Londonderry Aire

A-maz-ing grace shall al-ways be my song of praise, For it was grace that bought my lib-er-ty; I do not know just why He came to love me so, He looked be-yond my fault, and saw my need. I shall for-ev-er lift mine eyes to Cal-va-ry, To view the

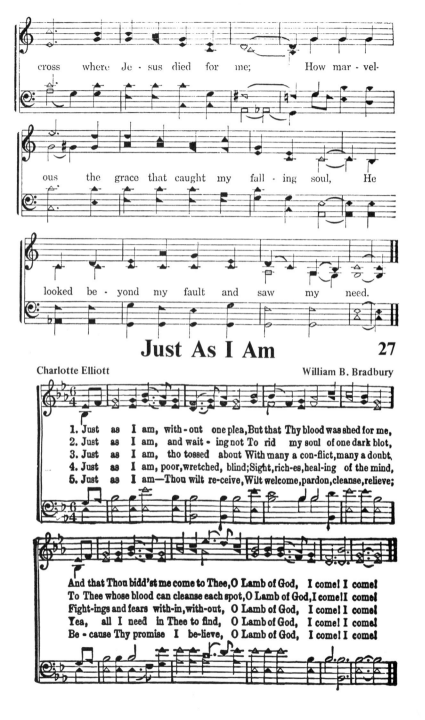

cross where Je-sus died for me; How mar-vel-

ous the grace that caught my fall-ing soul, He

looked be-yond my fault and saw my need.

Just As I Am

27

Charlotte Elliott

William B. Bradbury

1. Just as I am, with-out one plea, But that Thy blood was shed for me,
2. Just as I am, and wait-ing not To rid my soul of one dark blot,
3. Just as I am, tho tossed about With many a con-flict, many a doubt,
4. Just as I am, poor, wretched, blind; Sight, rich-es, heal-ing of the mind,
5. Just as I am—Thou wilt re-ceive, Wilt welcome, pardon, cleanse, relieve;

And that Thou bidd'st me come to Thee, O Lamb of God, I come! I come!
To Thee whose blood can cleanse each spot, O Lamb of God, I come! I come!
Fight-ings and fears with-in, with-out, O Lamb of God, I come! I come!
Yea, all I need in Thee to find, O Lamb of God, I come! I come!
Be-cause Thy promise I be-lieve, O Lamb of God, I come! I come!

28 Jesus Will Outshine Them All

G. J.

Gordon Jensen

REFRAIN

Man-sions will glis-ten on the Hills of Glo-ry, Happy re-unions on streets of gold, An-gel choirs singing glad prais-es for-ev-er But
Ah ———————————————————— yes

FINE   **VERSE**

Je-sus will outshine them all! 1. Oh, what glo-ry a-waits me
2. The sparkling riv-er is flow-ing,

— in Heav-en's bright cit-y, When I get there such sights I'll be-
Hap-py fac-es all glow-ing, Land of splen-dor where night nev-er

hold! A mil-lion scenes of rare beauty will de-mand that I
falls, The gold-en glass gives re-flection to that cit-ty's per-

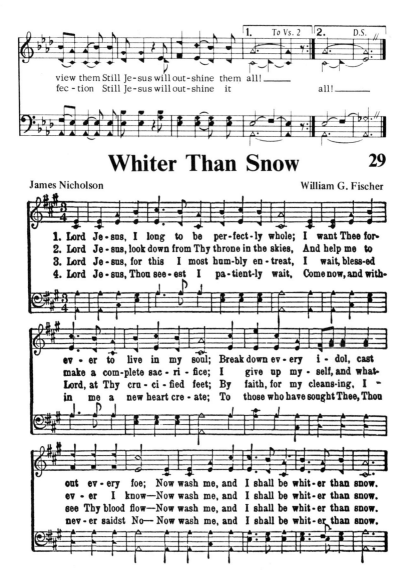

view them Still Je-sus will out-shine them all!_____
fec - tion Still Je-sus will out-shine it   all!_____

Whiter Than Snow

29

James Nicholson

William G. Fischer

1. Lord Je-sus, I long to be per-fect-ly whole; I want Thee for-
2. Lord Je-sus, look down from Thy throne in the skies, And help me to
3. Lord Je-sus, for this I most hum-bly en-treat, I wait, bless-ed
4. Lord Je-sus, Thou see-est I pa-tient-ly wait, Come now, and with-

ev - er to live in my soul; Break down ev-ery i-dol, cast
make a com-plete sac - ri - fice; I give up my-self, and what-
Lord, at Thy cru - ci-fied feet; By faith, for my cleans-ing, I -
in me a new heart cre - ate; To those who have sought Thee, Thou

out ev - ery foe; Now wash me, and I shall be whit-er than snow.
ev - er I know—Now wash me, and I shall be whit-er than snow.
see Thy blood flow—Now wash me, and I shall be whit-er than snow.
nev - er saidst No— Now wash me, and I shall be whit-er than snow.

CHORUS

Whiter than snow, yes, whiter than snow; Now wash me, and I shall be whiter than snow.

30 I've Never Loved Him Better

H. S.

Henry Slaughter

1. Since Je-sus came and found me and put His arms a-round me, And
2. Oh, bless-ed Friend Su-per-nal, my hope and joy e-ter-nal, Keep

all my bind-ing fet-ters took a-way. Al-though I've loved Him
Thou my soul 'til shad-ows flee a-way. For night-ly I would

dear-ly and trust-ed Him sin-cere-ly, I've nev-er loved Him
pray, Lord, 'Til end this pil-grim way, Lord,

CHORUS

bet-ter than to-day. I've nev-er loved Him bet-ter than to-day, I've

nev-er felt Him clos-er on the way: And oh! how sweet the feeling when

in His presence kneeling, I've never loved Him bet-ter than today.

What A Precious Friend 31

H. S.

Henry Slaughter

1. I've a Friend who's al-ways near me, I've a Friend who al-ways
2. On His prom-ise I'm re - ly - ing, All my needs He is sup-

cheers me; I've a Friend who is so dear to me,   What a pre-cious
ply - ing; He'll be there when I am dy - ing,

FINE   CHORUS

Friend is He!__   He'll go with me thru the val - leys. He'll go with me

D.S.

all the way__ Ev-'ry- day: Sav - iour, help me to have faith in Thee.

32 It Had To Be Love

H. L.

Harold Lane

33 God's Wonderful People

L.W.

Lanny Wolfe

REFRAIN: I love the thrill that I feel when I get to-geth-er with God's wonder-ful peo - ple, Love the thrill that I feel when I get to-geth-er with God's won-der-ful peo - ple; What a sight just to see all the hap-py fa-ces prais-ing God in heav-en-ly pla-ces; What a thrill that I feel when I get to-geth-er with

God's _____ won-der-ful peo - ple. _____

VERSE:

1. Oh, what joy His love _____ af-fords _____ when we meet in one _____
2. It can be just an - y-where _____ two or three are gath -
3. On that great re - un - ion day _____ when our Lord says, "Come __

ac - cord, _____ And we lift our hearts in praise __ un-to the Lord; _____
ered there, _____ That the Spir-it of the Lord __ will be there, too; _____
a - way", ___ And the saints from ev'ry land _ sweep thro' the gates; _____

There's no place I'd ra - ther be than with the ones who've been set free,
There's no fel - low-ship so sweet, __ there's no thrill that can compete
Join - ing loved ones 'round the throne, at last we'll all be gath-ered home,

D. C.

I'm so glad I'm in God's great _____ big fam - i - ly. _____
With the thrill I feel when-ev - er God's chil - dren meet. _____
That will be the great - est thrill __ we've ev - er known. _____

34 The Family Of God

Gloria & William J. Gaither

William J. Gaither

I'm so glad I'm a part of the fam-'ly of God; I've been washed in the foun-tain, Cleansed by His blood! Joint heirs with Je-sus as we tra-vel this sod, For I'm part of the fam-'ly

1-2 Going on the fam-'ly of God.

3 FINE God.

VERSE:

1. You will no - tice we say bro - ther _____ and sis - ter _____ 'round
2. From the door _____ of an orph -'nage to the house of _____ the

here, It's be - cause we're a fam - 'ly _____ and these
King, No _____ long - er an out - cast, _____ a _____

folks are so near. When one has a heart - ache _____
new song I sing; From rags un - to rich - es, _____

we _____ all share the tears, And re - joice _____ in each
from the weak to the strong, I'm not wor - thy _____ to

D. S.

vic - t'ry _____ in this fam - 'ly so dear. _____
be _____ here _____ but praise God I be - long! _____

35 Give Them All To Jesus

Bob Benson, Sr. & P. J.

Phil Johnson

1. Are you tired o' chas - in' _____ pret - ty rain - bows? ____
2. ____ He nev - er said ____ you'd on - ly see sun - shine, ____

And are you tired o' spin - nin'
And He ____ nev - er said ____ there'd

____ 'round and 'round? _____
be no ____ rain; _____

Wrap up all the shat -
____ He on - ly prom -

.......tered dreams _____ of your ____ life, ____
.........ised a heart full of sing - in', ____

And at the feet of Je - sus lay them down.
A - bout the ver - y things ____ that once brought pain. Give them

36 Jesus Got Ahold O' My Life

D. H.

Dallas Holm

REFRAIN:

D. C. Je - sus got a - hold o' my life ___ and He won't let me go!

Je - sus got in - to my heart, ___ He got in- to my soul! ___ I used to be ___ oh so sad,

But now I'm just - a free and glad, ___ 'Cause Je - sus got a- hold o' my life ___ and He won't let me go! ___

FINE

37
You're All Invited
To My Mansion

J. S.

John Stallings

1. In my life I've strug - gled _____ and I've oft known
2. If a flick - 'ring lamp you have _____ in place of

bit - ter tears; Rich - es have e - lud - ed me thro'
chan - del - liers, Board - ed floors may grace the home you've

all my _____ man - y years; _____ But some sweet day in
lived in _____ all these years; _____ Just be true to

Heav - en, a man - sion waits for me, And
Je - sus and some day when life is o'er, He's

I will o - pen wide its door through-out e - ter - ni -
prom - ised you a man - sion o - ver on the gold - en

CHORUS:

ty. _____
shore. _____ You're all _____ in - vit - ed to my man - sion; _____ Down here _____ I've nev - er had _____ much, tho' I al - ways tried to share; _____ But all _____ my doors _____ will be o - pen o - ver yon - der: You're in - vit - ed to my man - sion o - ver there. _____

38 Beautiful Scars

L. W. H.

L. Wayne Hilliard

Look at His hands, ___ they're nail-pierced; ___ Look at His

feet, ___ they're torn; ___ Look at His side, ___ it's riv-en; ___

And His brow, oh! He wore a crown of thorns. ___

And the world would look at the tor-ture, ___ And de-clare

it was on-ly a shame; ___ But the scars

39 The Resurrection Morn

William J. & Gloria Gaither

William J. Gaither

1. Oh, what a day! T'will soon take place, when the re-deemed of
2. God's might-y an-gel takes His stand, up-on the sea, and
3. Then sea and land give up their dead; the earth too long has
4. Then row on row they'll fall in line, their per-fect gar-ments
5. The might-y band will start to play the Hal-le-lu-jah

Ad-am's race, In an in-stant will __ all be transformed; __ They'll
on the land; And He sounds __ that __ great trum-pet blast; __ Then
been their bed; Re - leased, __ they __ rise through the air; __ They'll
snow-y white, They'll march in and __ claim their own land. __ "They're
Chorus that day; All __ glo-ry to the King of all Kings. __ Then

come from near, some from a - far, on past the moon, be-
like a thou-sand thun-ders roar, de - clares that time shall
join and come as mag-net drawn to gath-er 'round that
home at last!" the King will say; "These are my own, for
tears of joy will start to flow be-cause I've cho-sen

yond the stars; What a sight! On that great hap-py morn. __
be no more, worlds stop! For __ this day's the last. __
Great white throne, be - hold! Their __ King wait-ing there. __ The
these are they washed __ white in the blood of the Lamb." __
long a - go to be there when the Saints start to sing. __

CHORUS:

trump will sound; A - mens re - sound; The saints will rise up from the ground; Such sing - ing _____ and shout- ing _____ We've run the race, we'll see His face and start to sing A - maz - ing Grace; What a sight! On that Res - ur - rec - tion morn. _____

40 I'll Have A New Life

L. G. P.

Luther G. Presley

1. On the res-ur-rec-tion morn-ing when all the dead in Christ shall rise,
2. Free from ev-'ry im-per-fec-tion, youth-ful and hap-py I shall be,
3. What a hal-le-lu-jah morn-ing when the last trump of God shall sound,

Praise the Lord, I'll have a new life;
I'll have a new bod-y, e-ter-nal;

Sown in weak-ness, raised in pow-er, read-y to live in Par-a-dise,
Glo-ri-fied with Him for-ev-er, death will be lost in vic-to-ry,
Graves all burst-ing, saints a shout-ing, heav-en-ly beau-ty all a-round,

Praise the Lord I'll have a new life.
I'll have a new bod-y, O yes.

CHORUS

Glo-ry, glo-ry, nev-er sad,
I'll have a new home of love e-ter-nal with the re-deemed of God to stand,

There'll be no more sor-row, No more pain, there'll be no more strife;
no strife;

Yes, raised in the like-ness of my Sav-ior, read-y to live in glo-ry land,
In His like-ness, I'll be glad,

I'll have a new bod-y, Praise the Lord, I'll have a new life.
e-ter-nal.

Revive Us Again

41

Wm. P. Mackay

J. J. Husband

1. We praise Thee, O God, for the Son of Thy love, For Je-sus, Who died and is
2. All glo-ry and praise to the Lamb that was slain, Who has borne all our sins and has
3. Re-vive us a-gain, fill each heart with Thy love, May each soul be rekindled with

CHORUS

now gone above.
cleansed ev'ry stain. Hal-le-lu-jah! Thine the glory, Hallelujah! amen; Re-vive us a-gain.
fire from a-bove.

42
D. R.

Prisoner Of Love

Dottie Rambo

1. When I came to Je - sus, I set-tled it all; I gave Him my life to con-trol __ Nei-ther fear nor per-suasion could draw me to Christ, But His love __ has __ cap-tured my soul.

2. He holds me se-cure with his love strong and true; I'm hap-py His serv-ant to be __ In __ bondage to Je-sus for-ev-er I'll stay; My __ soul __ does-n't want to be free. __

CHORUS

I'm a pris-'ner of love __ a slave to the Mas-ter __ I will-ing-ly toil __ thro' the

I'm a pris-'ner of love
I will-ing-ly toil

heat and the cold _____ I seek no re-ward _____

I seek no reward

in this world be - low _____ But pay -day will

in this world be -low

come _____ when the pearl - y gates un - fold. _____

Give Me Oil In My Lamp 43

Unknown

Arr. by Adger M. Pace

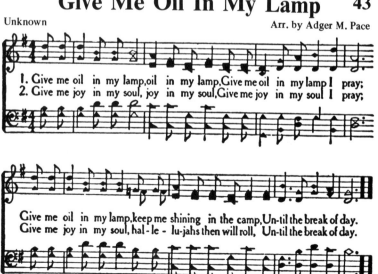

1. Give me oil in my lamp, oil in my lamp, Give me oil in my lamp I pray;
2. Give me joy in my soul, joy in my soul, Give me joy in my soul I pray;

Give me oil in my lamp, keep me shining in the camp, Un-til the break of day.
Give me joy in my soul, hal - le - lu-jahs then will roll, Un-til the break of day.

44 I Have Found A Hiding Place

Chas. F. Weigle

Gladys Blanchard Muller

1. I have found a hid-ing place when sore dis-trest, Je-sus, Rock of
2. I have found the sweet-est flow'r that ev-er grew, Je-sus, "Rose of
3. I have found a love-ly star that shines on high, Je-sus, "Bright and

A-ges, strong and true; In a wea-ry land I in His shad-ow rest,
Shar-on" fair and pure; He's my joy and com-fort, bless-ed Friend so true,
Morn-ing Star" to me; In the night of sor-row He is ev-er nigh,

He is my strength in all that I do.
He blooms with-in my heart ev-er-more.
He drives the dark-est shad-ows a-way.

CHORUS

Je-sus, "Rock of A-ges,"

let me hide in Thee; Je-sus, "Rose of Shar-on," sweet Thou art to me; "Lil-y

of the Val-ley," "Bright and Morning Star," Fairest of ten thousand to my soul.

Far Above The Starry Sky

45

T. S.

Theodore Sisk

1. Soon I'll leave this world of sor-row, For that home-land of the soul,
2. Soon I'll walk the streets of glo-ry, Meet with loved ones gone be-fore,
3. Come and go with me to glo-ry, From all sor-row we'll be free,

It will be a bright to-mor-row, When the pearl-y gates un-fold; Sav-ior,
O what shout-ing, O what sing-ing, When He o-pens wide the door; Christ Him-
Then we'll sing love's grand old sto-ry, Just a-cross the jas-per sea; With my

be Thou ev-er near me, Till I reach my home on high, Where I'll rest from
self will come to greet me, To that hap-py home on high, He will give to
harp and crown I'll ev-er Play the song "sweet by and by," With the hosts of

all my la-bor,
me a wel-come, Far a-bove the star-ry sky. 'Twill be glo-ry, hal-le-
Heav-en join-ing,

lu-jah, No, I'll nev-er know a sigh; In the hap-py new Je-ru-sa-lem,

46 (Jesus Will Be What Makes It) Heaven For Me

Ł. W.

Lanny Wolfe

1. I've heard of a land that is won-drous-ly fair, ___ They
2. If walls there weren't jas-per, if streets were not gold; ___ If

say that it's splen-dor is far be-yond com-pare; ___ In that
man-sions would crum-ble, if folks ___ there grew old; ___ Still I'd

place that's called Heav - en my ___ soul longs to be, ___ For
see ev - 'ry - thing, ___ I've been long-ing to see, ___ If

where Je - sus is, ___ It will be Heav-en for me.
Je - sus is there, ___ It will be Heav-en for me.

CHORUS:

Heav - en for me, Heav - en for me, Je - sus will

be what makes it Heav-en for me; ___ All its beau-ty and

won-ders I'm long-ing to see, ___ But Je-sus will

be ___ what makes it Heav-en for me.

Nearer, My God, To Thee 47

Sarah A. Adams

Lowell Mason

1. Near - er, my God, to Thee, Near-er to Thee; E'en tho' it be a cross,
2. Tho' like the wan - der - er, The sun goes down; Darkness be o - ver me,
3. There let the way ap-pear, Steps un-to heav'n; All that Thou send-est me,

D.S.—Near-er, my God, to Thee,

D. S.

That rais-eth me. Still all my song shall be, Near-er, my God to Thee,
My rest a stone. Yet in my dreams I'd be, Near-er, my God to Thee,
In mer-cy giv'n. An-gels to beck-on me, Near-er, my God to Thee,

Near - er to Thee.

48 Hide Me, Rock Of Ages

B. C. G.

Brantley C. George

1. O thou bless-ed Rock of A-ges,(Rock of A-ges, I am)Trust-ing
2. Keep me when the storm-clouds gath-er,(storm-clouds gather, keep me) Till the
3. When my jour-ney is com-plet-ed, (is com-plet-ed, Sav-ior,)And there's

now dear Lord in Thee;(dear Lord in Thee I'm trust-ing) Keep me till my
sun comes shin-ing thru;(comes shin-ing thru the shad-ows) Keep me till my
no more work to do; (no work to do, O bless-ed) Sav-ior guide my

D. S.-When the storm a-

FINE

jour-ney's end-ed,(jour-ney's end-ed, Keep me) Till Thy blessed face I see.
work is o-ver,(work is o-ver, Keep me) Till I bid this world a-dieu.
wea-ry spir-it, (wea-ry spir-it, To that) Hap-py land be-yond the blue.

round me rag-es,(round me rag-es, Bless-ed) Rock of A-ges hide Thou me.

CHORUS

Hide me, O blest Rock of A - ges,
A - ges, Rock of A - ges, hide me,

D. S.

Till Thy bless-ed face I see; (Thy face I see, in glo-ry)

Jesus Is His Name

49

W. E. M.

W. Elmo Mercer

1. There is One Who is with me As I walk down life's highway, Je-sus
2. When I cried out for mer - cy, There was One Who brought pardon, Je-sus

is His name; On His arm I am lean-ing, And on Him I'm de-
is His name; When I fell in my weakness There was One Who re-

pend-ing, Je - sus is His name. One who is lov - ing;
stored me, Je - sus is His name. (Ah)

One who is true; One who is watching All that I do; There is One who's forgiving,
(Oo)

This I know, Hal - le - lu - jah! Je - sus is His name.

50 Touching Jesus

J. S.   Cue notes for 2nd verse solo   John Stallings

1. A wom-an ___ tried man-y ___ phy-si-cians, ___
2. I was bound when I knelt at that old al-tar,

___ Yet grew worse, so to Je-sus she came;
But they said Je-sus could meet ev-'ry need; ___

___ And when the crowd tried ___ to re-strain her,
And when this pris-'ner fin- 'ly touched Je-sus,

___ She whispered these words thro' her pain: "Touching
He set me free, praise the Lord, free in-deed!

CHORUS

Je - sus is all ___ that mat-ters", ___

Then your life will nev - er be the same;

There is on - ly one way to touch Him,

Just be - lieve when you call on His name.

The Old-Time Religion   51

Arranged

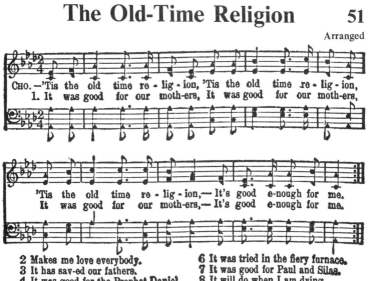

CHO.—'Tis the old time re - lig - ion, 'Tis the old time re - lig - ion,
1. It was good for our moth-ers, It was good for our moth-ers,

'Tis the old time re - lig - ion,— It's good e-nough for me.
It was good for our moth-ers,— It's good e-nough for me.

2 Makes me love everybody.
3. It has sav-ed our fathers.
4. It was good for the Prophet Daniel.
5. It was good for the Hebrew children.

6 It was tried in the fiery furnace.
7 It was good for Paul and Silas.
8 It will do when I am dying.
9 It can take us all to heaven.

52 Only Jesus Can Satisfy Your Soul

L. W.

Lanny Wolfe

1. The world will try to sat - is - fy___ that___ long - ing in your
2. If you could have the fame and for - tune, all the wealth you could ob-

soul, You may search the wide world o'er, ___ but you'll be just as be-
tain, Yet you have not Christ with - in, your liv - ing here would be in

fore! You'll nev - er find true sat - is - fac - tion ___ un - til you've
vain: There'll come a time when death shall call you, ___ rich - es can - not

found the Lord, For on - ly Je - sus___ ___ ___ can sat - is - fy your soul.
help you then, So come to Je - sus ___ for on - ly He can sat - is - fy.

CHORUS

Sat - is - fy your soul, on - ly Je - sus ___ can sat - is - fy your soul, _____
soul, sat - is - fy your

soul. And on-ly He — can change your heart and make you whole; —

He'll give you peace — you nev-er knew, — (sweet) love and joy —

and heav-en, too, For on-ly Je- sus — can sat-is-fy your soul! —

Doxology 53

Thomas Ken

Louis Bourgeois

Praise God, from whom all blessings flow; Praise Him, all crea-tures here be - low;

Praise Him a-bove, ye heav'nly host; Praise Father, Son, and Ho - ly Ghost.

54 I Wish You All Could Know Him

P. J.

Phil Johnson

1. __ If I had but one wish granted to me, __ If I
had __ just one dream, _____ And if I had the pow'r to
make this dream come true, I'd have the whole world know Him like I do.

2. If you would on-ly talk to Him __ one time, I'm sure your
wast-ed life would be all through; __ You would feel the full-ness
of His love, _____ And you'd be free to share it like I do.

CHORUS:

I wish you all __ would love __ Him like I love __ Him; __

I wish you all __ could see __ Him like I do; __ I wish you

all could feel ___ His sweet, sweet pres - ence _____

I wish you all could know ___ Him like I know ___ Him! ___

Only Trust Him

55

J. H. S.

J. H. Stockton

1. Come, ev - 'ry soul by sin op-pressed, There's mer-cy with the Lord,
2. For Je - sus shed His pre - cious blood, Rich bless-ings to be - stow;
3. Yes, Je - sus is the Truth, the Way, That leads you in - to rest;
4. Come, then, and join this ho - ly band, And on to glo - ry go,

And He will sure - ly give you rest By trust - ing in His word.
Plunge now in - to the crim - son flood That wash - es white as snow.
Be - lieve in Him with - out de - lay, And you are ful - ly blest.
To dwell in that ce - les - tial land, Where joys im - mor - tal flow.

Chorus

1 2

On - ly trust Him, on - ly trust Him, On-ly trust Him now; }
He will save you, He will save you, He will (Omit.......) } save you now.

56 Neither Do I Condemn Thee

W. Elmo Mercer

1. ____ By the crowd of wor-ship-ers, Sor - ry for their sins,
2. They told ____ of her wan -der-ings, Mak - ing each flaw,
3. ____ Still ____ cried the Phar - i - sees, "Pray, ____ Mas - ter, pray,
4. ____ Cheeks ____ flush - ing with the shame, Turn - ing a - bout,
5. ____ Spoke ____ He most ten - der - ly, "Pray, ____ wom - an, pray,

Was a poor ____ wan - der - er, Rude - ly brought in;
Spoke of her ____ pun - ish - ment, Quot - ing the law;
What shall we ____ do with her? What ____ doth Thou say?"
And from His ____ pres - ence, Walk - ing slow - ly out.
Hast Thou no ac - cu - sers?" "Nay, ____ Mas - ter, nay."

Scribes ____ came and Phar - i - sees, Anx - ious to see
Writ - ing up - on the ground, Sad - ly and slow,
Then ____ said He re - buk - ing - ly, "Let the first stone
Then ____ saw we stand - ing there, Head bend - ing low,
"Nei - ther do I con - demn ____ thee, Soul, sick and sore;

What ____ the meek Naz - a - rene's Ver - dict would be.
But said He un - heed - ing - ly, Head ____ bend - ly low:
Come ____ from the sin - less hands, Hence ____ and a - lone."
He ____ Who the world des - pised Bade her sin no more.
Go ____ forth, I par - don thee; Go and sin no more."

CHORUS:

"Nei - ther do I con - demn ____ thee," Prec - ious words di - vine; From the lips of mer - cy Like the sweet - est chimes. Won - der - ful words of Je - sus, Sing them o'er and o'er; "Nei - ther do I con - demn ____ thee, Go and sin no more."

57 Jesus Be The Lord Of All

L. W. & M. W.

Lanny & Marietta Wolfe

REFRAIN:

(1, 2 & 1st. D.S.) Je - sus be the Lord of all, Je - sus be the Lord of all,
(2nd. D.S.) Je - sus, I sur - ren - der all, Je - sus, I sur - ren - der all,

(Last time to ⊕) ⌐1

Je - sus be the Lord of all the king - doms of my heart. ___
Je - sus I sur - ren - der all the king - doms of my (to CODA)

⌐2 ___ VERSE:

heart. 1. In my heart ___ are king - doms of ___ a
2. I guess ___ I on - ly fooled my - self, for I

world that's ___ all my own; ___ King - doms
said I had yield - ed all; But in a se - cret corn-

that ___ are on - ly seen ___ by my - self and ___ God a-
___ er of my heart ___ was a king - dom that did not

58 Jesus (He Is The Son Of God)

D. L.

Danny Lee

1. The bus-y streets and side-walks, they sud-den-ly grew still, As a Man came thro' the en-trance of the ci-ty; As He touched and healed a blind man with a lit-tle piece of clay, With trem-bling lips you could hear the peo-ple say:

2. There are foot-prints in the sand a-long the Sea of Gal-i-lee Where thou-sands came to hear and came to see Him; There He taught of love and kind-ness, yes, He bro't a bet-ter way, As He spoke they'd turn and whis-per and they'd say:

3. Then the air grew cold and the sky turned black as they nailed Him to a tree, There He died for ev-'ry man and ev-'ry coun-try; But the price He paid and the blood He shed is chang-ing lives to-day, And with joy and praise you can hear these peo-ple say:

Je - sus, Je - sus, He is the Son of God! Je - sus, Je - sus, the prec - ious Son of God! ___ Sweet - est Rose of Shar - on came to set us free; Je - sus, Je - sus, He's ev - 'ry - thing to me; Yes, He's all the world ___ to me! ___

59 You Won't Believe The Difference

D. R.

Dave Redman

REFRAIN:

O, you won't be-lieve the dif-f'rence 'til you've tried Him

and you've found that your life has been made o-ver and new

hap-pi-ness a-bounds; 'Til you've known the joy of serv-ing

Him, felt His pres-ence ev-'ry day, O, you won't be-lieve the

Last time to ⊕   VERSE:

dif-f'rence 'til He's in your heart to stay! ___ If you could

60 There's Enough Of God's Love

G. J.

Gordon Jensen

(Cue notes for 2nd, Verse)

1. There's e - nough of God's love _____ to fill _____ the o - cean deep, There's enough of God's love _____ to scale _____ a mountain's peak, There's enough _____ of God's love to pass the high - est star, There's enough of God's love _____ to change a man's _ heart.

2. There's e - nough of God's love _____ to make liv - in' life _____ a real _____ joy, There's enough of God's love _____ all _____ ha - tred _____ could be des-troyed, If man-kind would on - ly try God's love for what it's worth, There's enough of God's love to bring peace _____ on _____ earth. _____

REFRAIN:

There's e-nough of God's love _____ for _____ an - y - one, _____

61 God's Family

L. W.

Lanny Wolfe

1. We're ___ part of the fam - 'ly that's been born a-
2. When a bro - ther meets sor - row we all feel his
3. And tho' some go be - fore ___ us, we'll all meet a-

gain; ___ ___ Part of the fam - 'ly whose
grief; ___ When he's passed thro' the val - ley we
gain; ___ ___ Just in - side the ci - ty as

love knows no end; ___ For Je - sus has saved ___
all feel re - lief; ___ To - geth - er in sun-
we en - ter in; ___ There'll be no more part-

us, and made us His own, ___ Now we're
shine, to - geth - er in rain, ___ To -
ing, with Je - sus we'll be ___ To -

part of the fam - 'ly that's on its way home. ___
geth - er in vic - t'ry through His prec - ious name. ___
geth - er for - ev - er, ___ God's fam - i - ly.

CHORUS:

And some-times we laugh ___ to-geth-er, some-times we cry; ___ Some-times we share ___ to-geth-er, ___ heart-aches and sighs; ___ Some-times we dream ___ to-geth-er of how it will be ___ When we all get to Heav - en, God's fam - i - ly. ___

62 When I Say Jesus

REFRAIN:

When I say "Mas-ter," My sor-rows dis-ap-pear; When I say "Fa-ther," He drives a-way my fears; When I say "Sav-ior," My blind-ed eyes can see; .... When I say "Je-sus," He speaks peace to me! me!

63
After Calvary

L. T.

LaVerne Tripp

1. Take my hand, _____ lead me thru dark-est val-leys, _____ Com-mand, _____ and I would go _____ a-cross the sea; _____ Just take my hand and guide _____ me, wher-e'er you'd have me be, I'd do an-y-thing, af-ter Cal-va-

2. _____ I'll stand up _____ and I'll dare to be dif-f'rent, _____ Un-a-shamed, _____ _____ I'll try _____ to live like Thee; _____ Lord, take my life and mold _____ me the way you'd have me be,

64 Let's Just Praise The Lord

W. J. G. & G. G.

William J. & Gloria Gaither

1. We ___ thank You for Your kindness, We thank You for Your love, We've
2. Just the pre-cious name of Je-sus is worth-y of our praise, Let us

been in heav'n-ly plac-es, felt bless-ings ___ from a-bove; We've been
bow our knee be-fore Him, our hands ___ to heav-en raise; When He

shar-ing all the good - things, the fam-'ly can af-ford, Let's just
comes in clouds of Glo - ry, with Him to ev - er reign, Let's ___

CHORUS:

turn our praise t'ward heaven, and praise ___ the Lord. Let's just praise ___ the
lift our hap-py voic-es, and praise His dear Name.

Lord! ___ Praise ___ the Lord! ___ Let's just lift our hands to heav-en and

praise___ the Lord; Let's just praise___ the Lord,___ praise___ the

Lord, ___ Let's just lift our hands t'ward heaven and praise the Lord. ___

Oh, How I Love Jesus

65

1. There is a name I love to hear, I love to sing its worth; It sounds like
2. It tells me of a Sav-ior's love, Who died to set me free; It tells me
3. It tells me what my Fa-ther hath In store for ev - 'ry day, And tho I
4. It tells of One whose loving heart Can feel my deepest woe, Who in each

CHORUS

mu - sic in mine ear, The sweetest name on earth.
of His pre-cious blood, The sinner's perfect plea. Oh, how I love Je-sus,
tread a darksome path, Yields sunshine all the way.
sor - row bears a part, That none can bear below.

Oh, how I love Je-sus, Oh, how I love Je-sus, Be-cause He first loved me!

66 More Than Enough

M. F. M. & W. E. M.

Marcia F. Mercer & W. Elmo Mercer

1. Some - times — when I fal - ter and stum-ble a - long, Blind-ly
2. When I search for hands to guide me a - long on my way, When I'm

grop-ing in the dark-ness I cre - at - ed all a - lone, Je - sus
need-ing for - give-ness and strength for the day, Then by

comes and takes the bur - den, Picks me up when I'm down, Oh, He
faith I go to je - sus, He a - lone under-stands, And He

an - swers my pray'r _____ And His mer - cies a-bound!
holds me se - cure - ly _____ In His al - might - y hands!

CHORUS

He gives me more than e-nough _____ More — than e - nough!

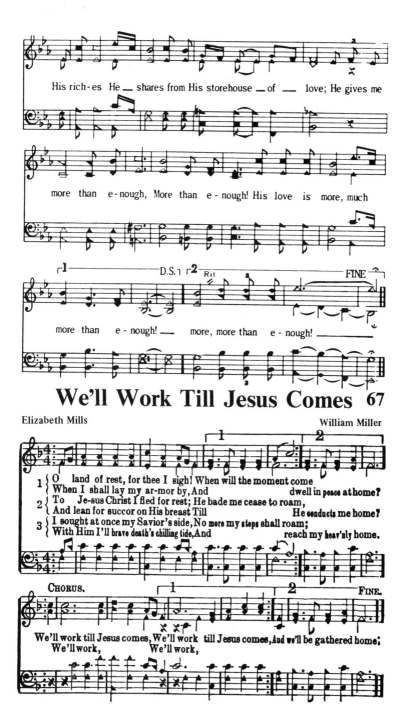

His rich-es He — shares from His storehouse — of — love; He gives me

more than e-nough, More than e - nough! His love is more, much

1 — **2** Rit — FINE

more than e - nough! — more, more than e - nough! —

We'll Work Till Jesus Comes 67

Elizabeth Mills

William Miller

1 { O land of rest, for thee I sigh! When will the moment come
When I shall lay my ar-mor by, And dwell in peace at home?

2 { To Je-sus Christ I fled for rest; He bade me cease to roam,
And lean for succor on His breast Till He conducts me home?

3 { I sought at once my Savior's side, No more my steps shall roam;
With Him I'll brave death's chilling tide, And reach my heav'nly home.

CHORUS. — **1** **2** FINE.

We'll work till Jesus comes, We'll work till Jesus comes, And we'll be gathered home;
We'll work, We'll work,

68 Do You Know My Jesus?

W. F. (Bill) Lakey & V. B. (Vep) Ellis

1. Have you a heart that's wea-ry, Tend-ing a load of care; Are you a soul that's seek-ing Rest from the bur-den you bear? Do you know my Je-sus, Do you know my friend, Have you heard He loves you, And that He will a-bide till the end?

2. Where is your heart, oh, pil-grim, What does your light re-veal; Who hears your call for com-fort When naught but sor-row you feel?

3. Who knows your dis-ap-point-ments, Who hears each time you cry; Who un-der-stands your heart-aches, Who dries the tears from your eyes?

CHORUS

Do you know my Je-sus, Do you know my friend, Have you heard He loves you, And that He will a-bide till the end? till the end?

Each Step I Take

69

W. E. M.

W. Elmo Mercer

1. Each step I take my Sav-iour goes be-fore me, And with His lov-ing hand
2. At times I feel my faith be-gin to wa-ver, When up a-head I see
3. I trust in God, no mat-ter come what may, For life e-ter - nal

He leads the way. And with each breath I whis-per "I a-dore Thee;" Oh, what
a chas-m wide, It's then I turn and look up to my Sav-iour, I am
is in His hand, He holds the key that o-pens up the way, That will

Rit.

CHORUS

joy to walk with Him each day.
strong when He is by my side. Each step I take I know that He will
lead me to the promised land.

guide me; To high-er ground He ev - er leads me on. Un-til some day the last

Rit.

step will be tak - en, Each step I take just leads me clos - er home.

When God Dips His Love In My Heart

70

C. D.

Cleavant Derricks

1. When God dips His pen of love in my heart And writes my soul a mes-sage He wants me to know, His Spir-it all di-vine fills this sin-ful soul of mine, When God dips His love in my heart.

2. Sometimes tho' the way is drear-y, dark and cold, And some un-burdened sor-row keeps me from the goal, I go to God in prayer, I can al-ways find Him there (hal-le-lu-jah!) To whisper sweet peace to my soul.

3. He walked ev-'ry step up Cal-v'ry's rug-ged way To give His life com-plete-ly, and bring a bet-ter day; My life was steeped in sin, but in love He took me in, His blood washed away ev-'ry stain.

REFRAIN

Well, I said I wouldn't tell it to a liv-ing soul How He bro't sal-va-tion when He made me

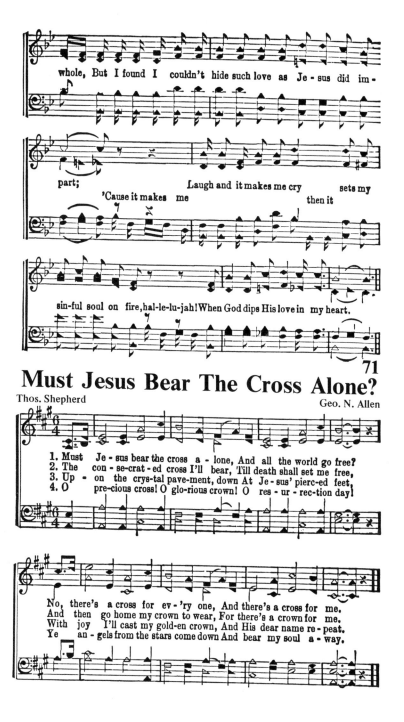

whole, But I found I couldn't hide such love as Je-sus did im-part;

'Cause it makes me   Laugh and it makes me cry   then it   sets my

sin-ful soul on fire, hal-le-lu-jah! When God dips His love in my heart.

71

Must Jesus Bear The Cross Alone?

Thos. Shepherd

Geo. N. Allen

1. Must Je-sus bear the cross a-lone, And all the world go free?
2. The con-se-crat-ed cross I'll bear, Till death shall set me free,
3. Up-on the crys-tal pave-ment, down At Je-sus' pierc-ed feet,
4. O pre-cious cross! O glo-rious crown! O res-ur-rec-tion day!

No, there's a cross for ev-'ry one, And there's a cross for me.
And then go home my crown to wear, For there's a crown for me.
With joy I'll cast my gold-en crown, And His dear name re-peat.
Ye an-gels from the stars come down And bear my soul a-way.

72 Whosoever Meaneth Me

J. E. M.

J. Edwin McConnell

1. I am hap - py to - day and the sun shines bright, The clouds have been
2. All my hopes have been raised, O His name be praised, His glo - ry has
3. O what won - der - ful love, O what grace di - vine, That Je - sus should

rolled a - way; For the Sav - ior said Who - so - ev - er will, May
filled my soul; I've been lift - ed up and from sin set free, His
die for me; I was lost in sin, for the world I pined, But

CHORUS.

come with Him to stay. (to stay.) "Who-so-ev-er," surely mean-eth me,
blood hath made me whole. (me whole.)
now I am set free. (set free.)

Sure - ly mean-eth me, O sure - ly mean-eth me; "Who-so - ev - er,"

sure - ly mean-eth me, "Who - so - ev - er," mean - eth me.
mean- eth me.

Where No One Stands Alone

73

M. L.

Mosie Lister

1. Once I stood in the night with my head bowed low, _____ In the
2. Like a king I may live in a pal-ace so tall, _____ With great

darkness as black as could be; And my heart felt a-lone, and I cried
rich-es to call _____ my own; But I don't know a thing in this whole

CHORUS

"Oh, Lord, don't hide your face from me." "Hold my hand all the way,
wide world that's worse than being a-lone.

Ev-'ry hour, ev-'ry day, From here to the great un-known; _____

Take my hand, Let me stand Where no one stands a - lone." _____

74 Press Along To Gloryland

James Rowe

Emmett S. Dean

1. O ransomed souls, with joyous song, Press a-long to Glo-ry-land;
2. The foe may rave, but Christ will save,
3. To join once more those gone before,
4. The crown to wear for - ev - er there, Press along

Ex - tol-ling grace that saves the race, Press along to Glo-ry - land.
The storm may sweep, but He will keep,
With saints to sing be - fore the King,
To sing His praise thru countless days, Press a-long

Chorus

Press a - long, glad soul, press a - long, Giv - ing
Press a - long,

out the mes-sage grand; Let -ting love, God's
Giv-ing out Let -ting love,

love, be your song, Press a - long to Glo - ry - land.
Press a - long

The Savior Is Waiting

75

R. C.

Ralph Carmichael

1. The Sav-ior is wait-ing to en-ter your heart. Why don't you let Him
2. If you'll take one step t'ward the Savior my friend, You'll find His arms o-

come in?___ There's noth-ing in this world to keep you a-part.
pen wide. ___ Re-ceive Him and all of your dark-ness will end.

REFRAIN

What is your an-swer to Him?___ Time af-ter time He has wait-ed
With-in your heart He'll a-bide.___

be-fore And now He is wait-ing a-gain. ___ To see if you're

will-ing to o-pen the door. Oh, how He wants to come in! ___

76 If That Isn't Love

D. R.

Dottie Rambo

1. He left the splen-dor of Heav-en ____ Knowing His des - ti-
2. E - ven in death He re-mem-bered ____ The thief hanging by His

ny ____ Was the lone-ly hill of Gol-goth-a ____ There to lay
side ____ ____ He spoke with love and compassion ____ Then He took

CHORUS Tacet

down His life for me. ____ If that is - n't love ____ The
him , to Par - a - dise. ____

o - cean is dry; ____ There's no stars in the sky ____ And the sparrow ____

Tacet

can't fly! ____ If that is - n't love ____ Then Heav-en's a

myth __ There's no feeling like this ___ If that is - n't love.___

A Child Of The King 77

Hattie E. Buell

Rev. John B. Sumner, arr.

1. My Fa-ther is rich in hous-es and lands, He hold-eth the wealth of the
2. My Fa-ther's own Son, the Sav-ior of men, Once wandered on earth as the
3. I once was an out-cast stranger on earth, A sin-ner by choice, and an
4. A tent or a cot-tage why should I care? They're building a pal-ace for

world in His hand! Of ru - bies and diamonds, of sil - ver and gold, His
poor - est of them. But now He is pleading our par - don on high, That
al - ien by birth; But I've been a-dopt-ed, my name's writ-ten down, An
me o - ver there; Tho' ex-iled from home, yet still I may sing: All

CHORUS

cof - fers are full, He has rich - es un - told.
we may be His when He comes by and by.
heir to a man-sion, a robe and a crown. I'm a child of the King, A
glo - ry to God, I'm a child of the King.

child of the King: With Je - sus my Sav-ior I'm a child of the King.

78 Is My Lord Satisfied With Me?

E. W. S.

E. W. (Bill) Sugge

1. One glo-r'ous day Je-sus came and made me whole, He so com-
plete-ly then sat-is-fied my soul; Now as I face life's dark trou-bled
storm-y sea, I won-der if He is sat-is-fied with me?

2. I'm sat-is-fied with God's great re-demp-tion plan I'm sat-is-
fied it's suf-fi-cient all for man; I'm sat-is-fied with His work on
Cal-va-ry, But is my Lord ful-ly sat-is-fied with me?

3. Lord give me strength, give me cour-age, make me bold That I might
lead some lost sheep in-to Thy fold; That I might stand un-a-fraid unmoved for Thee, That you might be ful-ly sat-is-fied with me.

CHORUS

I want my Lord to be sat-is-fied with me: I want my life to
be what He'd have it be; Then when I come to that great e-ter-ni-

ty, His smile will say He is sat-is-fied with me

sat-is-fied with me.

Is It Well With Your Soul? 79

James Rowe   Virgil O. Stamps

1. 'Mid the toil and strife of this bu-sy life, Is it well
2. Have you lost your sin, are you pure with-in?
3. Do you praise the love of the One a-bove? Is it well............

with your soul? Are you liv-ing right, should you die to-night?
Are you at the side of the Cru-ci-fied?
with your soul? Will the crown be won and the Lord's "well done?"

D.S.—Are you liv-ing right should you die to-night?

Fine   Chorus

Is it well with your soul? Is it well
Is it well   Is it well
Is it well............ witn your soul?

D.S.

with your soul, Are you free, glad and whole?
with your soul, Are you free, glad and whole?

80 It's In Your Hands

A. H.
Alton Harkins

1. Where's the spear that pierced His side When my Lord was cru-ci-fied? If you're
2. Where's the blood that from Him spilled That God's word might be fulfilled? If you're

not serv-ing Him, it's in your hands. Where's the nails that nailed Him there
not serv-ing Him, it's on your hands. Where's the crown of thorns He wore

As He died in deep despair? If you're not serving Him, it's in your hands.
As the cross for me He bore?

CHORUS

Christ is still the same; He feels ev-'ry pain when we dis-o-bey

His commands. Where's the ham-mer that drove the nails? If His

will now you've failed, I'm a-fraid, my friend, it's in your hands.

Hold To God's Unchanging Hand 81

Jennie Wilson

F. L. Eiland
Arr. by John T. Benson, Jr.

1. Time is filled with swift transi-tion, Naught of earth unmoved can stand, Build your
2. Trust in Him who will not leave you, What-so-ev-er years may bring, If by
3. Cov-et not this world's vain rich-es, That so rap-id-ly de-cay, Seek to
4. When your journey is com-plet-ed, If to God you have been true, Fair and

CHORUS

hopes on things e-ter-nal, Hold to God's unchanging hand! Hold
earth-ly friends for-sak-en, Still more close-ly to Him cling!
gain the heav'n-ly treas-ures, They will nev-er pass a-way!
bright the home in glo-ry, Your en-rap-tured soul will view! Hold to His hand,

to God's un-chang-ing hand! Hold   to God's un-chang-
Hold to His hand!

Rit.

ing hand! Build your hopes on things e-ter nal, Hold to God's unchanging hand!

82 Happiness

W. J. G.

William J. Gaither

CHORUS

I found hap-pi-ness, I found peace of mind, I found the joy of living, per-fect love sub-lime, I found real con-tent-ment, hap-py living in ac-cord, I found hap-pi-ness all the time, won-der-ful peace of mind when I found the Lord.

VERSE

1. No more lone-ly days of pain and mis-er-y, For the door of hap-pi-ness, I found the key;
2. I'm so hap-py with this brand new mel-o-dy, I have found that life can be a sym-pho-ny,

I have found a life of love and har-mo-ny, Won-drous hap-pi-
Look-ing for-ward to that hap-py ju-bi-lee, Glo-rious sym-pho-

ness all the time, har-mo-ny so di-vine, Since I found the Lord.
ny all the time, mel-o-dy so di-vine, Since I found the Lord.

Pass Me Not

83

Fanny J. Crosby

W. H. Doane

1. Pass me not, O gen-tle Sav-ior, Hear my hum-ble cry; While on oth-ers
2. Let me at a throne of mer-cy Find a sweet re-lief; Kneel-ing there in
3. Trusting on-ly in Thy mer-it, Would I seek Thy face; Heal my wounded
4. Thou the Spring of all my com-fort, More than life to me, Whom have I on

Chorus

Thou art call-ing, Do not pass me by.
deep con-trition, Help my un-be-lief. Sav-ior, Sav-ior, Hear my humble
brok-en spir-it, Save me by Thy grace.
earth beside Thee? Whom in heav'n but Thee?

cry; While on oth-ers Thou art call-ing, Do not pass me by.

84 One Day I Will

W. M. & J. S.

Walt Mills & John Stallings

(Cue notes for 2nd verse solo)

1. I have nev - er seen___ the face of my Sav - ior,___
2. From the time I first met Him He's been all to me,___

But serv-ing Him's_ been such a thrill!___ I have
And my life with His joy He has filled:___ And I'm

nev - er seen___ the gates to that cit - y: ___
long - ing for the day when my eyes shall be-hold Him:___

Oh, but one day,_ one day_ I will!___
Thank God! one day,_ one day_ I will!___

CHORUS

One day I'm gon-na

walk___ on streets of ___ pure gold: ___ And they

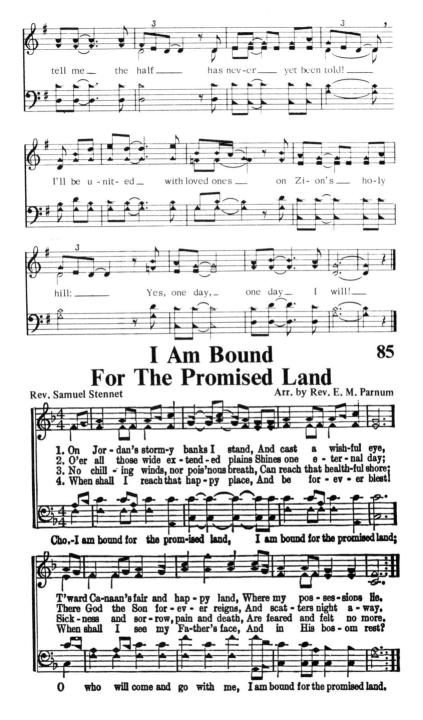

tell me___ the half___ has nev-er___ yet been told!___

I'll be u-nit-ed___ with loved ones___ on Zi-on's___ ho-ly

hill;___ Yes, one day,___ one day___ I will!___

I Am Bound
For The Promised Land

85

Rev. Samuel Stennet

Arr. by Rev. E. M. Parnum

1. On Jor-dan's storm-y banks I stand, And cast a wish-ful eye,
2. O'er all those wide ex-tend-ed plains Shines one e-ter-nal day;
3. No chill - ing winds, nor pois'nous breath, Can reach that health-ful shore;
4. When shall I reach that hap-py place, And be for - ev - er blest!

Cho.-I am bound for the prom-ised land, I am bound for the promised land;

T'ward Ca-naan's fair and hap-py land, Where my pos - ses-sions lie.
There God the Son for - ev - er reigns, And scat - ters night a - way.
Sick - ness and sor-row, pain and death, Are feared and felt no more.
When shall I see my Fa-ther's face, And in His bos - om rest?

O who will come and go with me, I am bound for the promised land.

86 I Don't Need To Understand

M. C.

Magdalene Crocker

1. Sun - shine comes and sun - shine goes; then shad - ows
2. Life is like a might - y sea, so tossed and
3. When my life down here is thru and Je - sus

lin - ger. Dark - ness fills the night with mys - te -
driv - en; Bil - lows rise with - in the heart of
calls me To my home up there up - on the

ry and care. But with - in my heart a gen - tle
ev - 'ry man. Storms so man - y times will leave the
gold - en shore, I'll look back, re - view the path that

voice re - minds me, "Fear no e - vil," Je - sus
heart with ques - tions That you don't need to un - der -
lay be - fore me; But I won't care to un - der -

CHORUS:

said, "for I'll be there."
stand; just hold His hand.   I don't need to
stand an - y - more.

87 Whatever It Takes

Lanny & Marietta Wolfe

Lanny Wolfe

1. There's a voice __ call-ing me from an old rug-ged tree, And it
2. Take the dear-est things to me, if that's how it must be __ To
3. Take my hous-es __ and lands, change my dreams and my plans, For I'm

whis-pers, __ "Draw clos-er to Me; _____ __ Leave this world
draw __ me _____ clos-er to Thee; _____ __ Let the dis-
plac-ing my whole life in your hands; _____ And if you call

far _____ be-hind, there are new heights _____ to climb,
.... ap-point-ments come, lone-ly days __ with-out the sun,
me _____ to-day to a land _____ far a-way,

CHORUS:

And a new place __ in Me you will find." __
If thro' sor-row more like You I'll be-come! For what-ev-er
Lord, I'll go _____ and Your will o-bey.

it takes to draw clos-er to You, Lord, That's what I'll be

88 It Can't Be Soon Enough For Me

H. S.

Henry Slaughter

1. I've heard for man - y, man - y years, ___ Je - sus
2. This world is full of greed, ___ lust and ha -
3. ___ Ev - en though I'm hap - py as a Chris -

is com - ing back; To take His chil - dren home with
tred we can see, Con - fu - sion rules and reigns it
tian ev - 'ry day, My life is full of hap - pi -

Him for all e - ter - ni - ty. ___ I've watched and
seems wher - ev - er you may go; ___ The prob - lems
ness, as much as one could know; ___ Still my heart's

seen the signs of His re - turn - ing for His own,
of this hour ___ there's no an - swer to be found,
filled with great an - ti - ci - pa - tion for that day!

And ___ it ___ can't be ___ soon e - nough for me. ___
Je - sus com - ing back is the on - ly hope I know. ___
When ___ Je - sus comes I'll ___ be so glad to go.

CHORUS:

And it can't be soon enough for Jesus to come back! To end all trouble we have come to know,___ The problems of this hour; There's no answer any-where, And His coming can't be soon enough for me.___ No, it can't be soon enough for me.___

89 Come On Down

Arr. by W. Elmo Mercer

Jack Hayford & Steve Stone

(1) The storehouse is full beyond measure, ____ The presses burst forth with new

wine, Your blessing is on us, Your word filled with promise, But one prayer fills

Begin slow rhythm · CHORUS:

this heart of mine: ____ Come on down, Lord Jesus, and take us away; Come on

down, ___ Lord Jesus, could this be the day? Even so, come quick-ly, Lord Je-sus, we

Last time to ⊕ Same tempo

pray; Come on down, Lord Jesus, come soon! ___ (2) He said, "Let not your hearts be

troubled,___ Tho' hearts all around fail with fear.   I'm coming to take you,

D. S. al Coda

I'll nev-er for - sake you; Look up! for my coming   is near."___ Come on

Coda

soon!   Take us home, Lord Jesus, Your church upward bring, "Maranatha" the

a tempo

word that our lips gladly sing; For we long to assemble before our great King; Come on

Broader

down, Lord Jesus, come soon;___   Come on down, Lord Je - sus,   come soon!___

90 Touring That City

H. L.

Harold Lane

1. Man-y times I have won-dered 'bout the sights of that
2. Here on earth we have trou-bles that to us seem so

cit-y, and __ all that my eyes shall be-hold; __ I will
heav-y, but in Heav-en no one will be sad; __ Mom and

see all the won-ders when I en-ter that cit-y there for-
Dad will be sing-ing, Heav-en's praise will be ring-ing for the

CHORUS:

ev-er to be safe in His fold. __
dear-est Friend __ I ev-er had. __ Some morn-ing you'll

find me tour-ing that cit-y, where the Son of God is the

91 I Came To Praise The Lord

W. J. G.   Spiritual

William J. Gaither

*1. I don't know what — you came to do,   but I came to praise —
2. I just came from a dear old — saint,   and she was — prais-ing
3. I just came from a "turned-on" — church,   and they were — prais-ing

*D. C. (Use 1st Verse)

the Lord, — I don't know what — you came to do,   but I came to
the Lord, — I just came from a dear old — saint,   and she was —
the Lord, — I just came from a "turned-on" — church,   and they were —

praise — the Lord; — I don't know what — you came to do,   but
prais-ing the Lord; — I just came from a dear old — saint,   and
prais-ing the Lord; — I just came from a "turned-on" — church,   and

I came to praise — the Lord, —
she was — prais-ing the Lord, — Hal - le - lu, — Hal - le - lu,
they were — prais - ing the Lord, —

┌ 1 - 2 - 3 ┐   ┌ FINE ending ┐

Hal - le - lu. _____ _____ Hal - le - lu. ____
Hal - le - lu.

You can sit a - round and complain, but I came to praise the Lord,
hum _____

You can sit and crit - i - cize all the saints, but I came to praise
hum _____

the Lord. _____ You can walk a - round with your nose in the air; You can
hum _____

crit - i - cize the way that I wear my hair; I don't know what
hum _____

D. C. al FINE

you came to do, but I ____ came to praise the Lord. ____

92 A Song To Sing At Midnight

G. J.

Gordon Jensen

1. _____ In my dark-est hour, my _____ lone-ly trou-bled hour, when_
2. From the jail _____ cell it rang as _____ Paul and Si - las sang;
3. An - y - one can sing a tune on a clear _____ day at noon; their re -

walk - in' by faith's the on - ly way, _____ _____ Lord, I'd ask of
Heav - en couldn't help but hear _____ their song; _____ Af - ter all they
lig - ion's not on trial, _____ not _____ at all; But, if they've got the

you one thing, and that would be a song to sing _____ till
had been through, _____ they were sing - in', they were true, _____ and
faith al - right, it's gon - na work _____ thro' the night, if they're still

CHORUS:

once a - gain I see the light of day! _____
right a - way the Lord sent help a - long. _____ Lord, _____ Give me a
sing - in' then they've got it af - ter all! _____

song to sing at mid-night _____ When trou - bles all a - round are

clos - in' in; ____ Lord, ____ Give me a song to sing at

(Sing cue notes for final ending)

mid - night: ____ If I ev - er need a song, dear Lord, it's then! ____

I Need Thee Every Hour 93

Mrs. Annie S. Hawks

Rev. Robert Lowry

1. I need Thee ev - 'ry hour, Most gra - cious Lord; No ten - der voice like
2. I need Thee ev - 'ry hour, Stay Thou near by; Temp-ta-tions lose their
3. I need Thee ev - 'ry hour, In joy or pain; Come quick-ly and a-
4. I need Thee ev - 'ry hour, Most Ho - ly One; O make me Thine in-

Chorus

Thine Can peace af - ford.
pow'r When Thou art nigh.   I need Thee, O I need Thee; Ev-'ry hour I
bide, Or life is vain.
deed, Thou bless - ed Son.

need Thee! O bless me now, my Sav - ior, I come to Thee!

94 Someday (It May Be Tomorrow)

D. L.

Danny Lee

1. I looked all a-round __ me __ and what could I see? __
2. There'll be no more tears __ nor __ __ say-ing good-bye, __
3. And then we'll see loved __ ones, __ __ pro-phets of old, __

A world filled with ha - tred __ and dark mis-er-y; __ We'll
We'll live in that man - sion __ __ built in the sky; __ And
__ walls made of ja - sper, __ __ streets of pure gold; __

Sin and con-fu - sion __ has ta-ken con-trol, __ __ Yet
rest 'neath the shade __ by __ the riv-er of life, __ __ And
Yet with all this __ still none can com-pare __ With a

CHORUS:

one ray of hope __ still __ beck-ons my soul. __
cease from our la - bor, __ toil __ and strife. __ Someday, __
glimpse of my Je - sus, __ His glo-ry to share. __

there'll be no more sor - row, __ Some-day, __ we'll walk hand

in hand; ___ Some-day, ___ it may be to-mor- row,

___ We'll walk to-geth ___ er thro' the prom ___ ised land. ___

I'm To The Highlands Bound 95

Charles P. Jones
C. P. J.
Arr. by John T. Benson, Jr.

1. My eyes are on the mountain top, I'm running for my life, I've left old Sodom
2. The an-gel voice has come to me, And cautioned me to go, And now o-be-dient
3. Some started with me and looked back, But forward yet I press; I'm bound to reach that

CHORUS

to the flames, With all its sin and strife.
to His word, I leave this land of woe. I'm to the high-lands bound, I'm
mountain top In ho - li - ness and peace.

seek-ing higher ground; I can't re-main in all the plain, I'm to the highlands bound.

96 Greater Is He That Is In Me

L.W.

Lanny Wolfe

REFRAIN:

D. C. Great-er is He ___ that is in me, Greater is He ___ that is in me, Greater is He ___ that is in me than he that is in ___ the world.

VERSE: (Cue notes for 2nd verse)

FINE

1. Sa - tan's like ___ a roar - ing lion ___ roam - ing to ___ and ___ fro, Seek - ing whom he may de - vour, ___ the Bi - ble tells me so; ___ Man - y souls have
2. On the ___ day of ___ Pen - te - cost ___ a rush - ing ___ might - y wind ___ Blew in - to the up - per room ___ and bap-tized all of them; ___ With a pow - er

been his prey —— to fall in some weak hour, —— But God has
great-er than —— —— an-y earth-ly foe, —— And I'm so

promised us to - day —— —— His o - ver - com-ing pow'r. ——
glad I've got it, too, —— —— I'm gon-na let the whole world know. ——

D. C.

There Is A Fountain

97

William Cowper   Lowell Mason

1. There is a foun-tain filled with blood Drawn from Im-man-uel's veins;
2. The dy-ing thief re-joiced to see That foun-tain in his day,
3. Dear dy-ing Lamb, Thy pre-cious blood Shall nev-er lose its pow'r,
4. E'er since by faith, I saw the stream Thy flow-ing wounds sup-ply,
5. Then in a no-bler, sweet-er song, I'll sing Thy pow'r to save,

Fine

D.S.—And sin-ners, plunged be-neath that flood, Lose all their guilt-y stains.
D.S.—And there may I, tho vile as he, Wash all my sins a-way.
D.S.—Till all the ran-somed church of God Be saved, to sin no more.
D.C.—Re - deem-ing love has been my theme, And shall be till I die.
D.S.—When this poor lisp-ing, stam'ring tongue Lies si - lent in the grave.

D. S.

Lose all their guilt-y stains, Lose all their guilt-y stains;
Wash all my sins a - way, Wash all my sins a - way;
Be saved, to sin no more, Be saved to sin 'no more;
And shall be till I die, And shall be till I die:
Lies si - lent in the grave, Lies si - lent in the grave;

98 Hallelujah Square

R. O.

Ray Overholt

1. Now I saw a blind man, tap - ping a - long, Los - ing his
2. Now I saw a crip - ple, drag - ging his feet, He could - n't
3. Now I saw an old man, gasp - ing for breath, Soon he'd be

way as he passed thru the throng; Tears filled my eyes, I said,
walk like we do down the street; I said, "My friend, I feel
gone as his eyes closed in death; He looked at me, said, "Boy,

"Friend you can't see", With a smile on his face, ___ he re-
sor - ry for you", But he said, "Up in heav - en I'm gonna
don't look so blue, I'm ___ goin' up to heav - en, ___

CHORUS:

plied ___ to me.
walk just like you." I'll see all my friends in Hal - le - lu - jah
how a - bout you?"

Square, What a won - der - ful time we'll all have up there; ___

We'll sing and praise Je - sus, His glo - ry to share, And you'll
And you'll
And we'll

not see one blind man
not see one crip - ple in Hal - le - lu - jah Square.
all live for - ev - er

The Great Physician

99

Wm. Hunter

J. H. Stockton

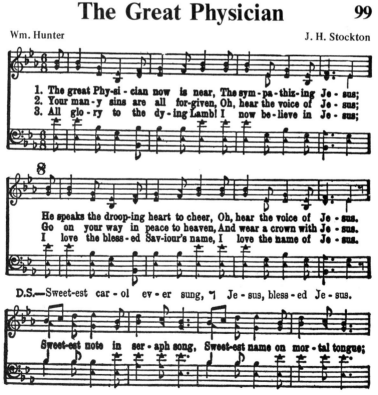

1. The great Phy-si - cian now is near, The sym - pa - thiz-ing Je - sus;
2. Your man - y sins are all for - given, Oh, hear the voice of Je - sus;
3. All glo - ry to the dy - ing Lamb! I now be - lieve in Je - sus;

He speaks the droop-ing heart to cheer, Oh, hear the voice of Je - sus.
Go on your way in peace to heaven, And wear a crown with Je - sus.
I love the bless - ed Sav-iour's name, I love the name of Je - sus.

D.S.—Sweet-est car - ol ev - er sung, Je - sus, bless - ed Je - sus.

Sweet-est note in ser - aph song, Sweet-est name on mor - tal tongue;

100 He's Still The King Of Kings

William J. & Gloria Gaither

William J. Gaither

1. In the hills of Ju - de - a the lone shep - herds watch;
2. He has walked by the grave - sides of earth's fall - en Kings;
3. When He rode thru the cit - y, the crowd claimed Him King;
4. At the sound of the trum - pet, the skies blaze with fire;

Hope is gone there is no call for sing - ing; ____ Then the
Who op - posed Him and yet He's still reign - ing; ____ Some - how
Thou - sands cheered and the streets filled with sing - ing; ____ But their
Moun - tains thun - der with God's judg - ment sing - ing; ____ But the

an - gels pro - claim that a Sav - ior is born, Hea - ven's lofts ech - o
love and com - pass - ion have con - quered it all, E - ven foes join with
song turned to curs - ing, the crown to a cross, They were blind to the
saints have no fear their Re - deem - er has come; Praise the Lord, thru all

CHORUS:

sweet Zi - on's ring - ing. ____
Heav - en pro - claim - ing. ____
wealth He was bring - ing. ____ Ho - san - na! Ho - san - na, The
a - ges, they're sing - ing. ____

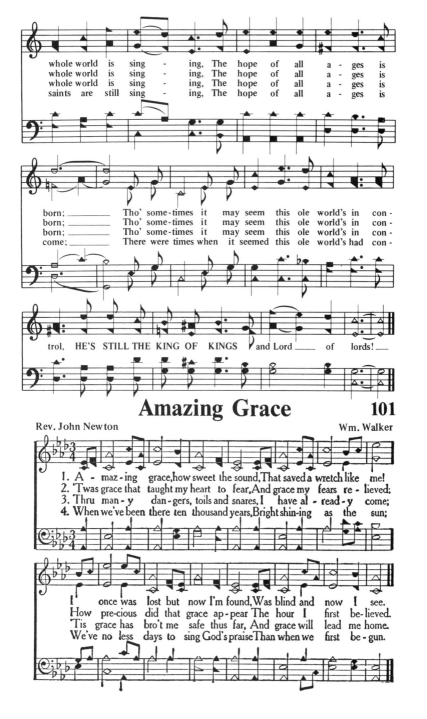

whole world is sing - ing, The hope of all a - ges is
whole world is sing - ing, The hope of all a - ges is
whole world is sing - ing, The hope of all a - ges is
saints are still sing - ing, The hope of all a - ges is

born; _____ Tho' some-times it may seem this ole world's in con -
born; _____ Tho' some-times it may seem this ole world's in con -
born; _____ Tho' some-times it may seem this ole world's in con -
come; _____ There were times when it seemed this ole world's had con -

trol, HE'S STILL THE KING OF KINGS and Lord _____ of lords! __

Amazing Grace 101

Rev. John Newton   Wm. Walker

1. A - maz - ing grace, how sweet the sound, That saved a wretch like me!
2. 'Twas grace that taught my heart to fear, And grace my fears re - lieved;
3. Thru man - y dan - gers, toils and snares, I have al - read - y come;
4. When we've been there ten thousand years, Bright shin-ing as the sun;

I once was lost but now I'm found, Was blind and now I see.
How pre-cious did that grace ap-pear The hour I first be - lieved.
'Tis grace has bro't me safe thus far, And grace will lead me home.
We've no less days to sing God's praise Than when we first be - gun.

102 I'll Be A Friend To Jesus

Rev. Johnson Oatman

J. W. Dennis

1. They tried my Lord..........and Mas-ter, With no one to ....de-
2. The world may turn..........a-gainst Him, I'll love Him to..........the
3. I'll do what He..........may bid me; I'll go where He..........may
4. To all who need..........a Sav-ior, My Friend I rec - - - om-

fend; With-in the halls......of Pi - late He stood without......a
end, And while on earth......I'm liv - ing, My Lord shall have......a
send; I'll try each fly - - ing mo-ment To prove that I'm......His
mend, Be-cause He bro't......sal - va-tion, Is why I am......His

Chorus

friend. I'll be a friend..............to Je - sus,
I'll be a friend to Je - sus,

My life for Him..............I'll spend; I'll be a friend..........
My life for Him I'll spend; I'll be a friend

to Je - sus, Un - til my years..............shall end.
to Je - sus, Un - til my years shall end.

There's Coming A Day

103

W. E. M.

W. Elmo Mercer

1. There's coming a day in God's tomorrow, When trials are past and hea-
2. The dawning will come and I'll see Je-sus Just waiting for me on hea-

ven's in view. No burdens to bear, no tears of sorrow, For God will be
ven's bright shore. I'll rush to His side and say, "Dear Master, I'm coming back

near to car-ry me through. The gates will o-pen and I shall enter
home to wander no more." O bliss-ful moment on yonder portals,

My home for-ev-er with Him to stay. What glo-ry 'twill be when I see
I'll praise my Je-sus, the Truth, the Way. Till then I will be a happy

Je-sus, My won-der-ful Lord, There's com-ing a day.
pil-grim, My jour-ney will end, There's com-ing a day.

104 The Old Gospel Ship

Arr. Alphus LeFevre

1. I have good news to bring and that is why I sing, All my joys with you
2. Oh, I can scarce-ly wait I know I'll not be late, For I'll spend my time
3. If you're ashamed of me you have no cause to be, For with Christ I am

I'll share; I'm going to take a trip in the Old Gos-pel ship
in pray'r; And when my ship comes in I will leave this world of sin
an heir; If too much fault you find you will sure be left be-hind

CHORUS

And go sail-ing thru the air.
And go sail-ing thru the air. Oh, I'm "gonna" take a trip, in the
While I go sail-ing thru the air.

good Old Gospel Ship, I'm go-ing far be-yond the sky; Oh, I'm "gonna"

shout and sing un-til the heavens ring, When I'm bidding this world good-bye.

Love Is Why

105

W. F. (Bill) Lakey & V. B. (Vep) Ellis

David Ellis & V. B. (Vep) Ellis

1. He nev-er said I'd have sil-ver or gold, Yet He has prom-ised me
2. I was a-stray full of sin with its shame, There was no peace with-in,
3. Tho' I have none of this world's precious goods, Yet I'm an heir to all

rich-es un-told; He nev-er suffered a life with-out care, Yet He re-
I was to blame; Tho' un-de-serv-ing, My life so de-filed, Now to my
Heav-en af-fords; Tho' I may nev-er a-chieve earth-ly fame, Yet all of

CHORUS

lieves ev'-ry bur-den I bear.
God I have been rec-on-ciled. Sin stained the Cross with the blood of my Lord,
Heav-en can call me by name.

Yet He per-mit-ted it with-out a word; Why, tell me why He re-

Rit. . . . .

deemed you and me? Love is why you and I are free.

106

I. S.

Room At The Cross

Ira Stanphill

With feeling

1. The cross up-on which Je-sus died Is a shel-ter in
2. Tho' mil-lions have found Him a friend And have turned from the
3. The hand of my Sav-iour is strong And the love of my

which we can hide, And its grace so free is suf-fi-cient
sins they have sinned, The Sav-iour still waits to o-pen
Sav-iour is long, Thro' sun-shine or rain thro' loss or

for me, And deep is its foun-tain; as wide as the sea.
the gates, And wel-come a sin-ner be-fore it's too late.
in gain, The blood flows from Cal-v'ry to cleanse ev-'ry stain.

CHORUS

There's room at the cross for you, There's room at the cross for you, Tho

millions have come There's still room for one, Yes, there's room at the cross for you.

The Longer I Serve Him

107

W. J. G.

William J. Gaither

1. Since I start - ed for the king-dom, Since my life He con - trols,
2. Ev - 'ry need He is sup - ply-ing, Plenteous grace He bestows,

Since I gave my heart to Je - sus, The longer I serve Him, the
Ev - 'ry day my way gets brighter,

CHORUS

sweet-er He grows. The long-er I serve Him, the sweeter He grows,

The more that I love Him, more love He bestows, Each day is like heaven, my

heart o - ver flows, The long-er I serve Him, the sweeter He grows.

108 Let Me Touch Him

V. B. E.

V. B. (Vep) Ellis

1. Let me touch Him, let me touch Jesus. ___ Let me touch Him
2. I was stray-ing so far from Je-sus, ___ I was lone-ly
3. There's a riv-er, a riv-er flow-ing. ___ From with-in ___

as He pass-es by; ___ Then when I shall reach out to oth-ers, ___
had no peace with-in; ___ Then the hand of my Sav-ior touch'd me, ___
and to cleanse my soul; And the flow sets my life to glow-ing. ___

CHORUS

They shall know Him, they shall live and not die. ___
Now I'm reach-ing to ___ oth-ers in sin. ___ Oh, to be His
Ho-ly spir-it, more than sil-ver and gold. ___

hand ex-tend-ed. ___ Reach-ing out to the op-press'd. Let me

touch Him, let me touch Jesus, ___ So that others may know and be bless'd.

Lonely Road! Up Calvary's Way 109

W. E. M.   W. Elmo Mercer

1. Up the Cal - va - ry way, Went my Sav-iour one day, With a heart that
2. Oh, the way Je - sus trod, Made a pathway to God, We can trav - el

was break-ing in two, Crown of thorns that He wore, Heav - y
the Cal - v'ry way, too, For this Je - sus in love, Leads to

Cross that He bore, — It was all for me and for you. —
Heav - en a - bove. If we fol - low His steps and are true.

CHORUS

Lone-ly road, Calv'ry's way was a lone - ly road to Je - sus that day;

Heav-y load, He bore our sins on that lone-ly road, Up Cal - va-ry's way.

110 Justified By Faith

G. J.

Gordon Jensen

1. Faith in Christ, no oth - er ____ Bears my soul t'ward
2. Could good works then save ____ me? ____ Christ did die in
3. Man - y ways are vaunt - ed, ____ And in Je - sus'

home; ____ All my try - ing o - ver, ____
vain! ____ Then would God's own glo - ry ____
name; ____ But God's word is fi - nal ____ The

God's way, His ____ a - lone! I'm just - i - fied by faith in
Oth - er's quick - ly ____ claim.
just shall live by ____ faith.

Je - sus, ____ Faith in Christ a - lone! ____ I'm just - i -

fied by faith in Je - sus, ____ Faith in Christ a - lone! ____

Bring Your Burden

111

L. R. I.

Lois R. Irwin

1. Why should I wor-ry or fear and dread, Al-though prob-lems un-
solved seem to be;— Can't you re-mem-ber what Jesus said? "Bring your
bur-dens and come to Me!"

2. Down in the val-ley through darkest night, Turn to Je-sus for
He is the Light;— Look 'round a-bout you and you will see He's the
Li-ly of your val-ley.—

3. He hears and an-swers each earn-est call, Tho' so wondrous I
know it is true;— He knows each sparrow and sees them fall, So He
sure-ly will care for you.—

CHORUS:

Hear Je-sus call-ing, "Come un-to Me; Come and I'll give you rest;— I'll give you rest; Bring ev-'ry bur-den, I'll set you free; Bring your bur-dens and come to Me!"—

112 That Glad Reunion Day

A. M. P.

Adger M. Pace

1. There will be a hap-py meet-ing in heav-en I know,
2. There with-in the ho-ly cit-y we'll sing and re-joice,
3. When we live a mil-lion years in that won-der-ful place,

When we see the ma-ny loved ones we've known here be-low,
Prais-ing Christ the bless-ed Sav-iour with heart and with voice,
Bask-ing in the love of Je-sus, be-hold-ing His face,

Gath-er on the bless-ed hill-tops with hearts all a-glow,
Tell Him how we came to love Him and make Him our choice,
It will seem but just a mo-ment of prais-ing His grace,

D. S.-There with all the ho-ly an-gels and loved ones to stay,

FINE   CHORUS

That will be a glad re-un-ion day.   Glad   day,   a
                                        That will be a hap-py day, yes, a

That will be a glad re-un-ion day.

D. S.

won-der-ful day, Glad   day,   a glo-ri-ous day;
won-der-ful day, That will be a hap-py day, yes, a glo-ri-ous day;

The Gloryland Way

113

J.S.T.

J. S. Torbett

1. I'm in the way, the bright and shin-ing way, I'm in the glo-ry land
2. List to the call, the gos-pel call to-day, Get in the glo-ry land
3. On-ward I go, re-joic-ing in His love, I'm in the glo-ry land

way;
glo-ry land way;
get

Tell-ing the world that Je-sus saves to-day, Yes,
Wand'rers,come home,oh, hast-en to o-bey, And
Soon I shall see Him in that home a-bove, Oh,

CHORUS

I'm in the glo-ry land way.
I'm

glo-ry land way

I'm in the glo-ry land

way,
glo-ry land way,

I'm in the glo-ry land way;
glo-ry land way;

Heav-en is

near-er, and the way groweth clearer, For I'm in the glo-ry land way.
glo-ry land way.

114 Let My Light Shine

D. H.

Dallas Holm

REFRAIN:

Let my ___ light shine in the night-time, Let it shine ___

___ all day through; Let it shine, ___ shine for Je-sus, ___

FINE   VERSE:

May it shine, ___ shine on you. ___   1. I was ___ walk-ing ___
2. Now I'm ___ liv-ing ___

a-long in the dark-ness,   I did-n't know ___ which way to
for just one ___ pur-pose: ___   To let the Lord ___ shine thro'

go; ___   Then the Lord, ___   He turned the Light on; ___   He changed
me; ___   If His love ___   can shine on oth-ers, ___   ___ Then

my ___ life _____ and saved my soul. ___ So let my ___
His ___ Spir - it _____ can set them free. ___

Bring Them In

115

Alexcenah Thomas

W. A. Ogden

1. Hark! 'tis the Shepherd's voice I hear, Out in the des - ert dark and drear,
2. Who'll go and help this Shepherd kind, Help Him the wand'ring ones to find?
3. Out in the des - ert hear their cry, Out on the mountains wild and high;

Call - ing the sheep who've gone astray, Far from the Shepherd's fold a - way.
Who'll bring the lost ones to the fold, Where they'll be sheltered from the cold?
Hark! 'tis the Mas - ter speaks to thee, "Go find My sheep wher-e'er they be."

CHORUS

Bring them in, bring them in, Bring them in from the fields of sin;

Bring them in, bring them in, Bring the wand'ring ones to Je - sus,

116

Come Into The Ark

G. J.

(Slowly with feeling)

Gordon Jensen

1. On __ Cal - va - ry's hill an ark has been built, __ Cost - ing the blood of God's Son! __ With it's door o - pen wide, there is saf - ty in - side, An - y - bod - y who will may get on. __

2. Untold thousands have heard, and heeding the word They have walked up the ramp called God's Grace; From the darkness of night in - to bless - ed new light, __ In - to the Sav - ior's em - brace. __

3. Soon to one and to all will go the last call, Then the door of God's mer - cy shall close; __ Op - por - tun - i - ty then will come nev - er a - gain, How __ soon 'twill be, on - ly God knows. __

CHORUS:

Come in - to the ark, Oh, the sky grows dark! There's a storm called God's Great Judgment Day; __

(mp) Ah __

From it's fierce, an - gry waves in the

Day; __

ark you'll be saved;_____ Come in - to the ark to - day!____
saved;

Higher Ground

117

Johnson Oatman, Jr.

Chas. H. Gabriel
Arr. by John T. Benson, Jr.

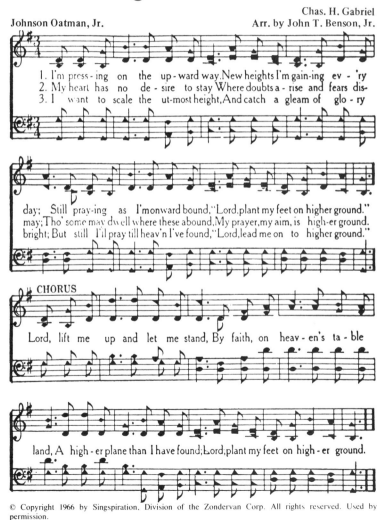

1. I'm press - ing on the up - ward way, New heights I'm gain-ing ev - 'ry
2. My heart has no de - sire to stay Where doubts a - rise and fears dis-
3. I want to scale the ut-most height, And catch a gleam of glo - ry

day; Still pray-ing as I'm onward bound, "Lord, plant my feet on higher ground."
may; Tho' some may dwell where these abound, My prayer, my aim, is high-er ground.
bright; But still I'll pray till heav'n I've found, "Lord, lead me on to higher ground."

CHORUS

Lord, lift me up and let me stand, By faith, on heav - en's ta - ble

land, A high - er plane than I have found; Lord, plant my feet on high - er ground.

118 He Restoreth My Soul

D. R.

Dottie Rambo

1. When I'm low in spir-it I cry Lord lift me up, I
2. It's dark as a dun-geon and the sun sel-dom shines, And I

want to go high-er with Thee; But the Lord knows I can't
ques-tion Lord, why must this be; But He tells me there's

live on the moun-tain, So He picked out a val-ley for me.
strength in my sor-row, And there's vic-t'ry in tri-als for me.

CHORUS

He leads me be-side still wat-ers, Some-where in the
still-wat-ers,

val-ley be-low; He draws me a-side to be tes-ted and

tried, But in The val·ley, HE RE-STOR-ETH MY SOUL.

Hiding In Thee

Rev. William O. Cushing

Ira D. Sankey

1. O safe to the Rock that is high·er than I, My soul in its
conflicts and sor·rows would fly; So sin·ful, so wea·ry, Thine, Thine
would I be; Thou blest Rock of A·ges, I'm hid·ing in Thee.

2. In calm of the noon-tide, in sor·row's lone hour, In times when temp-
ta·tions cast o'er me its pow'r; In tem·pest of life, on its wide
heav-ing sea, Thou blest Rock of A·ges, I'm hid·ing in Thee.

3. How oft in the con·flict, when pressed by the foe, I've fled to my
Ref·uge and breathed out my woe; How oft·en, when tri·als like sea-
bil·lows roll, I've hid·den in Thee, O Thou Rock of my soul.

Chorus

Hid·ing in Thee, Hid·ing in Thee,

Thou blest Rock of A·ges, I'm hid·ing in Thee.

120 Redemption Draweth Nigh

G. J.

Gordon Jensen

1. Years of time have come and gone since I first heard it told, How Jesus would come a - gain some day; If back then it seemed so real, then I just can't help but feel How much clos - er His com - ing is to - day.

2. Wars and strife on ev - 'ry hand, and vio - lence fills our land, Still some peo - ple doubt He'll come a - gain; But the word of God is true, He'll re - deem His chos - en few, Don't lose hope, soon Christ Je - sus will de - scend.

CHORUS

Signs of the times are ev - 'ry-where. And there's a brand-new feel - ing in the air; Keep your eyes up - on the

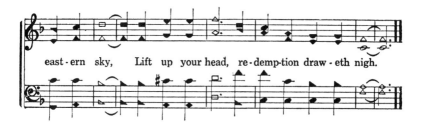

east-ern sky, Lift up your head, re-demp-tion draw-eth nigh.

God Be With You

121

J. E. Rankin

W. G. Tomer

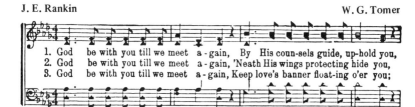

1. God be with you till we meet a-gain, By His coun-sels guide, up-hold you,
2. God be with you till we meet a-gain, 'Neath His wings protecting hide you,
3. God be with you till we meet a-gain, Keep love's banner float-ing o'er you;

With His sheep se-cure-ly fold you; God be with you till we meet a-gain!
Dai-ly man-na still pro-vide you; God be with you till we meet a-gain!
Smite death's threat'ning wave before you; God be with you till we meet a-gain!

CHORUS.

Till we meet,..... till we meet, Till we meet at Je-sus' feet;
Till we meet, till we meet a-gain, till we meet;

Till we meet,..... till we meet, God be with you till we meet a-gain!
Till we meet, till we meet again,

122 Some Glad Day

W. M. R.

Will M. Ramsey
Arr. by John T. Benson, Jr.

1. O bless-ed tho't......sweet rest will come,....Some glad day
2. These heav-y loads.......we shall lay down,....
3. Our suff'ring too........will soon be past,......
4. All war and strife.......will soon be o'er.

Some glad day

aft - er while; When all our toil....... on earth is done,......
When we re - ceive...... our heav'nly crown,.....
When we shall find......sweet rest at last,......
aft - er while; We'll find sweet peace..... on heaven's shore,......

CHORUS

There'll come a glad day aft - er while. O aft - er
aft - er while.

while, aft - er while, There'll come a glad day
Aft - er while, aft - er while,

aft - er while; O aft - er while, aft - er while,
aft-er while; Aft-er while, aft - er while,

There'll come a glad day aft-er while.

aft - er while.

I Feel Like Traveling On   123

Wm. Hunter, D. D.

Arr. by James D. Vaughan

With feeling.

1. My heav-'nly home is bright and fair, I feel like trav-el-ing on,
2. Its glit-t'ring-tow'rs the sun out-shine, I feel like trav-el-ing on,
3. Let oth-ers seek a home be-low, I feel like trav-el-ing on,
4. The Lord has been so good to me, I feel like trav-el-ing on,

Nor pain, nor death can en-ter there, I feel like travel-ing on.
That heav'nly mansion shall be mine, I feel like travel-ing on.
Which flames devour, or waves o'erflow, I feel like travel-ing on.
Un-til that bless-ed home I see, I feel like travel-ing on.

REFRAIN.

Yes, I feel like trav-el-ing on, I feel like trav-el-ing
trav-el-ing on,

on; My heav'nly home is bright and fair, I feel like traveling on.
travel-ing on;

124 Sorry, I Never Knew You

Sherman Branch

Henkle M. Little
Arr. by Jeffie Steele

1. Last night as I was sleep-ing, this dream came to me; I
2. I thought the time had come when I must stand the trial, I
3. There was my wife and chil-dren, I heard each one's voice, They
4. When I from sleep a-wak-ened, with tears in my eyes, I

dreamed a-bout the end of time a-bout e-ter-ni-ty; I
told the Lord that I had been a Chris-tian all the while; But
must have all been hap-py, it seemed they did re-joice, With
looked a-round, and there a-bout me, to my great sur-prise, I

saw a mil-lion sin-ners fall on their faces to pray, The Sav-ior
through the book He then looked, and sad-ly shook His head; They placed me
robes of white a-round them, and crowns up-on their head; My lit-tle
saw my wife and ba-bies, and knew I'd had a dream, Then down be-

CHORUS

sad-ly shook His head, and this I heard him say; Sor-ry, I ne-ver
o-ver on His left, and this is what He said; Sor-ry, I ne-ver
girl looked up at me, and this is what she said; Dad-dy, we can't go
side my bed I fell, and for mer-cy did scream; Fa-ther, Who art in

knew you, de-part from me for ev-er more; Sor-ry, I
knew you, I find no re-cord of your birth; Sor-ry, I
with you, We must stay on this love-ly shore; Sor-ry, for
glo-ry, In mer-cy look on me to-day; For-give me

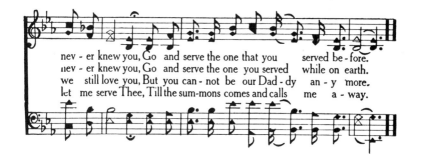

nev - er knew you, Go and serve the one that you served be - fore.
nev - er knew you, Go and serve the one you served while on earth.
we still love you, But you can - not be our Dad - dy an - y more.
let me serve Thee, Till the sum-mons comes and calls me a - way.

No, Not One

125

Johnson Oatman, Jr.

Geo. C. Hugg

1. There's not a friend like the low - ly Je - sus,
2. No friend like Him is so high and ho - ly,
3. There's not an hour that He is not near us, No, not one! no, not one!
4. Did ev - er saints find this Friend for-sake Him?
5. Was e'er a gift, like the Sav-ior giv - en?

Fine

None else could heal all our soul's dis - eas - es,
And yet no friend is so meek and low - ly,
No night so dark but His love can cheer us, No, not one, no, not one!
Or sin - ner find that He would not take him?
Will He re - fuse us a home in heav-en?

D.S.—There's not a friend like the low-ly Je - sus, No, not one, no, not one!

Chorus

D.S.

Je - sus knows all a - bout our strug-gles, He will guide till the day is done,

126 Ten Thousand Years

E. C.

Elmer Cole

1. Soon I'll come to the end of my jour-ney, And I'll meet the
2. We will just be-gin to sing love's sweet sto-ry, It's a song

one who gave His life for me: I will thank Him for the love
that the an-gels can-not sing: "I'm re-deemed by the blood

that He gave me, And ten thou-sand years or more I'll reign with
of the Sav-ior", And ten thou-sand years or more I'll praise His

CHORUS

Him. Ten thousand years we'll just be started, ten thou-sand
name.

years we've just be-gun: The bat-tle's o-ver and the

UNISON

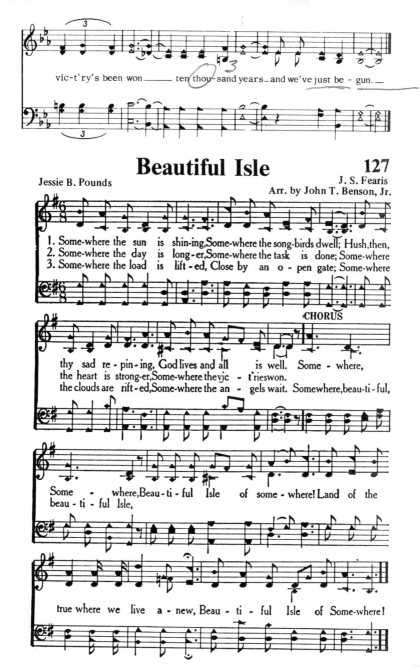

vic-t'ry's been won_____ ten thou-sand years_ and we've just be - gun. _

Beautiful Isle

127

Jessie B. Pounds

J. S. Fearis
Arr. by John T. Benson, Jr.

1. Some-where the sun is shin-ing,Some-where the song-birds dwell; Hush,then,
2. Some-where the day is long-er,Some-where the task is done; Some-where
3. Some-where the load is lift-ed, Close by an o-pen gate; Some-where

CHORUS

thy sad re-pin-ing, God lives and all is well. Some - where,
the heart is strong-er,Some-where the vic - t'ries won.
the clouds are rift-ed,Some-where the an - gels wait. Somewhere,beau-ti-ful,

Some - where,Beau-ti-ful Isle of some - where! Land of the
beau - ti - ful Isle,

true where we live a - new, Beau - ti - ful Isle of Some-where!

128   Joy, Real Joy

Words of 3rd verse by Gloria Gaither

William J. Gaither

*Cue notes for 3rd. Verse

1. For years I had longed for con - tent-ment, ___ ___ For years I had
2. I know what it means to be hap - py, ___ I know what it
* 3. I'm drinking at life's flow-ing foun-tain, ___ know the joy that all

longed for sweet rest, ___ But ___ now I have found a rich fountain, ___
means to have joy, ___ My ___ soul finds con - tent-ment in Je - sus, ___
heav'n can af - ford, For I've found a rich Gar - den of E - den, ___

CHORUS:

My ___ soul is so hap - py and blest. ___
That ___ noth-ing on earth can de - stroy. — JOY, REAL JOY, God's wonderful
And com-mune there with Je - sus my Lord. ___

joy is flood - ing the depths of my soul, _____ A joy that brings

peace and con-tent-ment, _____ God's won - der - ful, won - der - ful JOY. ___

Even So, Lord Jesus, Come 129

William J. & Gloria Gaither

William J. Gaither

1. In a world of fear and tur-moil, ___ In a race that seems so hard to run; ___ Lord I need Thy rich in-fill-ing, ___ Ev - en so, Lord Je - sus come. ___

2. When my eyes shall span the riv - er, ___ When I gaze in - to the vast un - known; ___ May I say with calm as - sur-ance, ___ "Ev - en now, Lord Je - sus come". ___

CHORUS:

EV - EN SO LORD JE - SUS, COME, ___ My heart doth long for Thee, ___ Tho' I've failed and be - trayed Thy trust, ___ EV - EN SO, LORD JE - SUS, COME. ___

130 The Old Rugged Cross

Solo and Chorus

Rev. George Bennard

1. On a hill far a-way stood an old rug-ged cross, The emblem of suf-f'ring and shame, And I love that old cross where the dear-est and best For a world of lost sin-ners was slain.

2. Oh, that old rug-ged cross, so despised by the world, Has a wondrous at-trac-tion for me, For the dear Lamb of God left His glo-ry a-bove, To bear it to dark Cal-va-ry.

3. In the old rug-ged cross, stained with blood so di-vine, A won-drous beau-ty I see; For 'twas on that old cross Je-sus suf-fered and died, To par-don and sanc-ti-fy me.

4. To the old rug-ged cross, I will ev-er be true, Its shame and re-proach glad-ly bear; Then He'll call me some day to my home far a-way, Where His glo-ry for-ev-er I'll share.

CHORUS

So I'll cher-ish the old rug-ged cross, the old rug-ged cross, Till my trophies at last I lay down; I will cling to the old rug-ged cross, the old rug-ged cross, And exchange it some day for a crown.

Mansion Over The Hilltop

131

I. S.

Ira Stanphill

1. I'm sat-is-fied with just a cot-tage be-low, A lit-tle sil-ver
2. Tho' of-ten tempt-ed tor - ment-ed and test-ed And like the proph-et
3. Don't think me poor or de - sert-ed or lone-ly, I'm not dis-couraged,

and a lit - tle gold; But in that cit-y where the ransomed will shine,
my pil-low a stone; And tho' I find here no per-manent dwelling,
I'm heav - en bound, I'm just a pil-grim in search of a cit-y,

CHORUS

I want a gold one that's sil - ver lined.
I know He'll give me a man-sion my own.
I want a man-sion, a harp and a crown.

I've got a mansion just

o - ver the hill - top, In that bright land where we'll never grow old, And some day

yonder we will nev-er-more wander But walk the streets that are purest gold.

132 The Way That He Loves

W. E. M.

W. Elmo Mercer

1. The way that He loves is as fair as the day, That bless-es my
2. The way that He loves is as deep as the sea, His spir-it shall

way with light. The way that He loves is as soft as the
my stay. The way that He loves is as pure as a

breeze, Ca-ress-ing the trees at night. So ten-der and pre-cious is
rose, Much sweet-er He grows each day. His peace hov-ers near like a

He, Con-tent-ed with Je-sus I'll be. The way that He
dove, I know there's a heav-en a-bove. To Je-sus I

loves is so thrill-ing be-cause His love reach-es e-ven me.
cling life's a won-der-ful thing Be-cause of the way He loves.

The Time Is Now

133

W. E. M.

W. Elmo Mercer

1. Pa - tient - ly Je - sus is call - ing you, Let noth - ing stand in
2. Life ev - er - last - ing is of - fered you, God will for - give ev -

your way ___ Think of the cost: e - ter - nal - ly lost! But you can be
'ry sin ___ Trust and be - lieve, sal - va - tion re - ceive The mo - ment you

CHORUS a tempo

saved to - day. The time is now, the Lord is here, Won't you
let Him in.

o - pen your heart while He is near; His will o - bey, oh don't

1 D.C. 2 FINE

de - lay! For sure - ly the time is now... now.

134 He Whispers Sweet Peace

W. M. R.
Will M. Ramsey

1. Some-time when mis-giv-ings dark-en the day, And faith's light I
2. I could not go on with-out Him I know, The world would o'er
3. I trust Him through faith, by faith hold His hand, And sometimes my
4. He speaks in a still, small voice we are told, A voice that dis-

can-not see; I ask my dear Lord to bright-en the way, He
whelm my soul; For I could not see the right way to go, When
faith is weak, And then when I ask Him to take com-mand, It
pels all fear; And when I'm in doubt, or trou-bled in soul, That

REFRAIN

whis-pers sweet peace to me. He whis-pers sweet peace to
temp-ta-tions o'er me roll. Yes He
seems that I hear Him speak.
still small voice I can hear.

me,.......... He whis-pers sweet peace to me,.......... When
whis-pers to me, He whis-pers sweet peace to me,

I am cast down in spir-it and soul, He whispers sweet peace to me.

O I Want To See Him

135

R. H. Cornelius
Arr. by R. E. Winsett

R. H. C.

1. As I jour-ney thru the land sing-ing as I go, Point-ing souls to
2. When in serv-ice for my Lord dark may be the night, But I'll cling more
3. When in val-leys low I look t'ward the mountain height, And be-hold my
4. When be-fore me bil-lows rise from the might-y deep, Then my Lord di-

Cal-va-ry, to the crim-son flow, Man-y ar-rows pierce my soul
close to Him, He will give me light; Sa-tan's snares may vex my soul,
Sav-ior there, lead-ing in the fight, With a tender hand outstretched
rects my bark, He doth safe-ly keep, And He leads me gen-tly on

FINE

from with-out, with-in; But my Lord leads me on, thru Him I must win.
turn my tho'ts a-side; But my Lord goes a-head, leads what-e'er be-tide.
t'ward the val-ley low; Guid-ing me, I can see, as I on-ward go.
thru this world be-low; He's a real friend to me, O I love Him so.

D. S.-Cares all past, Home at last, ev-er to re-joice.

CHORUS

O I want to see Him, look up-on His face, There to sing for-ev-er

D. S.

of His sav-ing grace; On the streets of Glory let me lift my voice;
His saving grace;

136
When My Savior
Reached Down For Me

G. E. W.

G. E. Wright

1. Once my soul was a-stray from the heav-en-ly way, And was wretch-ed and
2. I was near to de-spair when He came to me there, And He showed me that
3. How my heart does rejoice when I hear His sweet voice In the temp-est, to

vile as could be; But my Sav-ior in love gave me peace from a-bove,
I could be free; Then He lift-ed my feet, gave me gladness complete,
Him I then flee, There to lean on His arm, safe, se-cure from all harm,

Chorus

1-2 When He reached down His hand for me.   When my Savior reached down for
3 Since He   for me.

me,   When my Sav-ior reached down for me;   I was lost and un-
    for me,   for me;

done, without God or His Son, When my Sav-ior reached down for me.
                                                              for me.

Beautiful Star Of Bethlehem 137

Adger M. Pace   Theme by R. F. B.   R. Fisher Boyce   Har. by A. M. P.

1. Oh, beau-ti-ful Star of Beth-le-hem, shin-ing a-far thru shad-ows dim,
2. Oh, beau-ti-ful Star, the hope of light, guid-ing the pil-grim thru the night,
3. Oh, beau-ti-ful Star, the hope of rest, for the redeemed, the good and blest,

Giv-ing a light for those who long have gone, have gone; And guiding the wise men
O-ver the mountain till the break of dawn, the dawn; And in-to the light of
Yonder in glo-ry when the crown is won, is won; For Je-sus is now that

D.S.— Oh, give us thy light to

on their way un-to the place where Je-sus lay,
per-fect day it will give out a love-ly ray, Beau-ti-ful Star of Beth-le-
Star di-vine, brighter and brighter He will shine.

light the way in-to the land of per-fect day,

FINE. CHORUS.

hem shine on.   Oh, beau-ti-ful Star of
shine on.   Beau-ti-ful, beau-ti-ful Star,

D. S.

Beth-le-hem,   Shine up-on us un-til the glo-ry dawn;
Star of Beth-le-hem,   glo-ry dawn;

138 I Won't Have To Cross Jordan Alone

Thomas Ramsey

Chas. E. Durham

1. When I come to the riv-er at end-ing of day, When the last winds of
2. Of-ten-times I'm for-sak-en, and wea-ry and sad, When it seems that my
3. Tho' the bil-lows of sor-row and trouble may sweep, Christ the Sav-iour will

1. When the last

sor-row have blown; There'll be some-bod-y wait-ing to show me the way,
friends have all gone; There is one tho't that cheers me and makes my heart glad,
care for His own; Till the end of the jour-ney, my soul He will keep,
winds of sor-row have blown;

CHORUS

I won't have to cross Jor-dan a-lone. I won't have to cross Jor-dan a-
I won't have to cross
lone. Je-sus died for my sins to a-tone; When the
Jor-dan a-lone,

SOLO ad lib. PARTS

dark-ness I see, He'll be waiting for me, I won't have to cross Jordan a-lone.
Hum Hum

I Will Serve Thee

William J. & Gloria Gaither

William J. Gaither

I will serve Thee be-cause I love Thee, You have giv-en life to me; I was noth-ing be-fore You found me, You have giv-en life to me. Heart-aches, bro-ken piec-es, Ru-ined lives are why You died on Cal-v'ry; Your touch was what I longed for, You have giv-en life to me.

140 Promises

D. R.

Dottie Rambo

1. He didn't promise that I would nev-er stum-ble, But He did say He'd
2. He didn't promise my cross would not be heav-y, But He did say that

be there if I fall;_____ He_ didn't tell_ me He'd hear com-
He__ my load would share;_____ He_ didn't tell_ me He'd grant my

plaints I whis-per But He did say He'd hear me if I call._____
hopes and wish-es, But He did say He'd hear my earn-est pray'r._____

CHORUS

Prom-is-es,_____ Prom-is-es, And all of them_ true; He's done ex-

act-ly what He said He would do! He___ did-n't tell_ me my

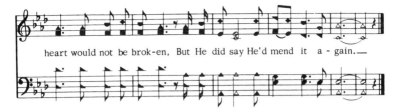

heart would not be brok-en, But He did say He'd mend it a-gain.—

Blessed Assurance 141

Fanny J. Crosby

Mrs. Joseph F. Knapp

1. Bless-ed as-sur-ance, Je-sus is mine! O what a for-taste of
2. Per-fect sub-mis-sion, per-fect de-light, Vi-sions of rap-ture now
3. Per-fect sub-mis-sion, all is at rest, I in my Sav-iour am

glo-ry di-vine! Heir of sal-va-tion, pur-chase of God,
burst on my sight. An-gels de-scend-ing bring from a-bove,
hap-py and blest. Watch-ing and wait-ing, look-ing a-bove,

FINE CHORUS

Born of His Spir-it, washed in His blood.
Ech-oes of mer-cy, whis-pers of love. This is my sto-ry, this is my song,
Filled with His goodness, lost in His love.

D. S.-Prais-ing my Sav-iour all the day long.

D.S.

Prais-ing my Sav-iour all the day long; This is my sto-ry, this is my song,

142 Lovest Thou Me?

William J. Gaither

William J. Gaither

1. Mod - ern times have brought us man - y com - forts, ___ Peo - ple
2. I love Thee more than this old world can of - fer, ___ All sin - ful

live in wealth and lux - u - ry; ___ But ___ the Mas - ter still asks this
fol - lies I de - ny for Thee; ___ My love, my life, ___ my all, I

ques - tion, ___ Lov - est thou Me, lov - est thou Me, more ___ than these? ___
pledge Thee, ___ I love Thee, Lord, I love Thee, Lord, more ___ than these! ___

CHORUS:

Lov - est thou Me, more than these, my child, What will your answer be? ___

O pre - cious Lord, I love Thee more than all of these, More ___ than fame,

more —— than wealth, —— more than the world. ——————

More than fame, wealth, the world. ——

I Know Whom I Have Believed 143

Daniel W. Whittle (El Nathan)

James McGranahan

1. I know not why God's wondrous grace To me He hath made known,
2. I know not how this sav-ing faith To me He did im-part,
3. I know not how the Spir-it moves, Con-vinc-ing men of sin,
4. I know not when my Lord may come, At night or noon-day fair,

Nor why, un-wor-thy, Christ in love Re-deemed me for His own.
Nor how be-liev-ing in His Word Wrought peace with-in my heart.
Re-veal-ing Je-sus thro' the Word, Cre-at-ing faith in Him.
Nor if I'll walk the vale with Him, Or "meet Him in the air."

CHORUS

But "I know whom I have be-liev-ed, and am per-suad-ed that He is

a-ble To keep that which I've com-mit-ted Un-to Him a-gainst that day."

144 I'll Glory In The Cross

G. J.

Gordon Jensen

1. A Man, a cross, a hill, a death so long a - go;
2. The nails, the spear, the whip, the thorns, the mock-er - ry,

What could it mean to me ___ a - cross the cen-tu - ries? ___ His
The un-told ag - o - ny, ___ He bore it will-ing-ly; ___ His

love, His plan, His grace, His wounds, the crimson flow: How could
hands, His feet, His side, His back, His brow, for me They took

CHORUS:

it transform me? ___ oh, pre-cious myster - y! ___ I'll glo - ry
sin's pen - al - ty, ___ se-cured my lib -er - ty! ___

in Cal - va - ry's tree: A symbol of death that means life to me. ___ I'll glo -

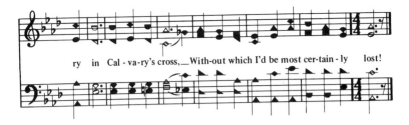

ry in Cal-va-ry's cross,—With-out which I'd be most cer-tain-ly lost!

I Remember Calvary 145

J. M. Black
Arr. by John T. Benson, Jr.

W. C. Martin

1. Where He may lead me I will go, For I have learned to trust Him
2. O I de - light in His com-mand, Love to be led by His dear
3. On - ward, I go, nor doubt nor fear, Hap-py with Christ my Sav - ior

so, And I re-mem-ber 'twas for me, That He was slain on
hand; His di - vine will is sweet to me, Hal-lowed by blood-stained
near, Trust-ing that I some day shall see Je - sus my Friend of

CHORUS

Cal - va - ry. Je - sus shall lead me night and day, Je - sus shall lead me all the

way, He is the tru - est Friend to me, For I re-mem-ber Cal - va - ry.

146 Before I Found The Lord

L.W.

Lanny Wolfe

1. I nev-er felt like this ___ be-fore, ___ I nev-er
2. I can't for-get those wast - ed years, ___ ___ All the

knew such bliss be - fore, ___ I nev-er had real peace be-fore ___ I
heart-aches and the tears, ___ All ___ hope seemed gone before ___ I

found the Lord; _____ I can't ex-plain just how ___
found the Lord; _____ But then He turned my life ___

I feel, ___ But, praise God, I know that it's real; ___ I nev-er
a-round, ___ Now my soul is heav-en ___ bound; ___ ___ All be-

CHORUS:

felt like this be-fore ___ I found the Lord. ___
cause one day I fin - al - ly found the Lord. ___ And now I've got ___

147 All In The Name Of Jesus

S. R. A.

Stephen R. Adams

1. Truth ___ and beau - ty ___ and hap - pi - ness,
2. Care ___ and com - fort, ___ ___ heal - ing and grace,

It's all ___ in the name ___ of Je - sus; ___

Health ___ and Heav - en, ___ ___ a peace ___ and rest, It's ___
Wel - come, ___ par - don, ___ a hid - ing place, ___

all ___ in the name ___ of Je - sus; ___ Joy ___ and
Warmth ___ and

glad - ness, ___ for - give - ness, too; ___ Life ___ ev - er -
sun - shine, ___ ___ friend - ship true; Ful - fill - ment ___ and

last - ing and free; ___ All ___ that I've longed for and
bless - ing un - told; ___ Hope ___ for to - mor - row and

all ___ I need, It's all ___ in the name ___ of
help for to - day,

CHORUS:

Je - sus. ___ Je - sus, Je - sus, He's here

and He will show you the way; ___ Je - sus, Je -

sus, He's all ___ that you need ___ to - day. ___

148 If It Keeps Gettin' Better

W. J. G.

William J. Gaither

(Chorus) If He keeps on bless-in' and bless-in', If He keeps on
(Verse) When I gave my heart to Je - sus, When I claimed Him

pour-in' it on,— If His love just keeps gettin' rich-er, If He keeps
as— my King,— When the gloom and fear—— was lift-ed, My ol' heart

on giv-in' a song;— If my cup gets full-er and full - er, If my
just start-ed to sing;— Then the song just kept— get-tin' big-ger, And it

prayers keep on get - tin' through If it keeps gettin' bet-ter and bet- ter,
thrilled my heart through and through

D.S. 2 *Special Chorus*

oh Lord, I don't know what I'm gon-na do!— — If He keeps on blessin'
Keeps

and bless - in',   If He keeps on pour-in' it on,_
on   bless-in' and bless-in',   Keeps   on   pour-in' it on,_

If His love just keeps get-tin' rich - er,   If He keeps on
Love   just   keeps get-tin' rich-er,   Keeps_

giv-in' the song;_   If my cup gets full-er and full - er,
_____   on   giv-in' the song,   Cup   gets   full-er and

If my   prayers keep on get-tin' through,   If it
full-er,   Prayers   keep   on get-tin' through

Fine

keeps get-tin' bet-ter and bet - ter, oh Lord, I don't know what I'm gonna do!_

149 You're Gonna Love Your New Life

P. J.

Phil Johnson

1. Someone told me some-thing a - bout you, And I must ad -
2. No more walk-ing thro' life with a frown, Your whole world has

mit I hope it's true; _____ They say that you fin - ally came a -
been turned up - side down; _____ No more search-ing for re - al - i -

round, _____ And a brand new life in Christ you found!
ty, _____ Truth is yours as you can plain - ly see.

Well, let me be the first to shake your hand, And tell you that this
_____ No more lone - ly days of emp - ti - ness, _____ On - ly per - fect

life is real - ly grand; _____ Sun - shine so much bright - er,
peace and hap - pi - ness; _____

Your load so much light-er, You're gon-na love___ your

CHORUS:

new life with the Lord! You're gon-na love___ your new life with the

Lord, It's like noth-ing that you've found be-fore; ___

No more tears and no more sor-row, No more wor-ries a-

bout to-mor-row, You're gon-na love___ your new life with the Lord!

150 Here Comes The Bride

R. M.

Ruth Munsey

1. What a cel - e - bra - tion on ___ that day, ___ It ___
2. Some from ev - 'ry na - tion will ___ be there, ___ Dressed in

can't be ver - y far ___ a - way; ___ When Heaven's Bridegroom
spot-less robe ___ so bright ___ and fair; ___ All of Heav - en

shall des - cend, ___ The ran-somed Church of ___ God ___ as - cend,
will be - hold, ___ The Bride ___ marching down the streets ___ of gold,

Heav - en's bells ___ will ___ sweet-ly ring, ___ Choirs of
We're ___ read - y wait-ing now to go, ___ The ver - y

an - gels ___ start to sing, ___ Pick up your trum-pet
hour ___ no one seems to know, ___

CHORUS:

Gab - r'el and blow. _____ Here comes the Bride to be ev - er at His

side; _____ The robe is spot-less white, _____ O what a

glo - ri - ous sight, _____ Here come the cho - sen ones,_____ Here

come the rap-tured ones, _____ An - gels step a - side, Here comes the Bride,_____
Here

An - gels step a - side, Here comes the Bride. _____
comes the Bride,

151 Oh, What A Happy Day

J. W. C.

Jack W. Campbell

1. Oh, what a hap-py time that's sure to be when my
2. And when I walk in-to heav-en fair, I'll see my

Je - sus is com-ing af - ter me, I hear Him call-ing me a-
bless - ed Sav - ior there, He'll place a crown upon my

way from this ol' world for - ev - er to stay; And when I
head, give me a robe of white to wear; I'll walk on

take my Sav-ior's hand in that bless - ed prom-ised land, I'll shout and
streets of pur-est gold, I'll live for-ev - er and not grow old,

sing through the end-less a - ges Oh, what a hap -py day.

CHORUS

Oh, what a hap-py day, that will be when we
What a hap-py day,

gath-er there, Oh what a hap-py day when we
What a hap-py day,

climb those gold-en stairs, We'll meet with those who have gone be-

fore, James and John and a mil-lion more, What a hap-py

time that's sure to be, Oh, what a hap-py day,
What a hap-py day.

152 Nearer To Thee

W. E. M.

W. Elmo Mercer

pray   near - er to Thee.
Yes, day aft - er day near - er to Thee, near - er to Thee.
lead   near - er to Thee.
Yes, they will all lead near - er to Thee, near - er to Thee.

CHORUS

Near-er to Thee,   Near-er to Thee,   O, blessed
Near-er to Thee, Nearer to Thee, Nearer to Thee,

Lord, This is my plea;   I long to
O, bless - ed Lord, This is my plea, This is my plea;

stand   in heav-en's fair land;
Yes, Lord, I'm longing to stand in heav-en's fair land, in heav-ens fair land;

Where I will be   near - er to Thee.
Lord, where I will be near - er to Thee, nearer to Thee.

153 I've Been To Calvary

W. J. G.

William J. Gaither

1. I've nev-er trav-eled far a-round the world,___
2. I walked the Cal-v'ry road, Where Je-sus trod,___

I've nev-er seen the man-y thrills and sights un-furled;___
I saw Him hang-ing___ there, The Son of God;___

But I have tak-en _____ the jour-ney of
With tear-stained __ eyes __ I knelt and prayed, "Je-sus

jour-neys for me, Up Cal-v'ry's Moun-tain there my
hear _____ my plea," Oh, praise the Lord, I'm glad I've

CHORUS:

Sav-ior _____ to see.___ I've been to Cal-va-
__ been __ to Cal-va-ry.___

154 Look For Me

S. P., Jr.

Squire Parsons, Jr.

1. If I leave this world of sor-row sometime be-fore you do, Just look for me in Hea-ven, and we'll talk the a-ges thru; But if, at first, you fail to see me, let me tell you where I'll be, I'll be thank-ing Christ, my Sav-ior, for sav-ing a

2. But if you should reach that cit-y be-fore my time has come, Per-haps you'd like to greet me when my race down here is run; Just wait, for I'll soon be com-ing a-cross life's ebb-ing sea, And I'll tell you now, my broth-er, just where to

CHORUS:

wretch like me. __ Don't __ look 'neath the gates of pearl, __ don't
wait for me. __ Don't __ wait 'neath the gates of pearl, __ don't

look on the streets of gold, __ Don't look by the walls of jas - per, __
wait on the streets of gold, __ Don't wait by the walls of jas - per, __

nor a - mong the man - y sights un - told; __ For I've been long - ing and

I've been wait - ing __ for the prec - ious, ho - ly One to meet, __

There I'll be thru the countless a - ges, __ look for me at Je - sus' feet. __
There I'll be thru the countless a - ges, __ wait for me at Je - sus' feet. __

155
C. M.

The Brush

Chuck Milhuff
Arr. by Harold Lane

Life started out like a can-vas, __ And God started painting on me, __ But I

took the paint brush from Jesus, and painted what I wished to see; The colors I

paint-ed kept running, __ And the ob-jects were all out of size, __ I had made a mess

of my painting, __ My way now seemed so unwise. Ooo __ Ooo __ So I

brought my painting to Jesus, __ All the col-ors, all the piec-es, so wrong, __ In the

markets of earth it was worthless, But His blood made my painting belong. He worked with no condemnation, Never mentioned the mess I had made, Then He dipped His brush in the rainbow, And He signed it, "The price has been paid." When I gave the brush back to Jesus, _____ When I gave the brush back to Him, He start-ed all o-ver life's can-vas to fill, When I gave to Je-sus, the brush of my will. _____

156

There Is A Light

P. J.

Phil Johnson

1. There is   a Light, _____   a Light that shines___ in the
   There is   a Song, _____   a Song that makes you want to
2. There is   a Light, _____   a Light that chas-es all the
   There is   a Song, _____   ___Ring-ing in the hearts of

dark - est night,   A Light that turns ___ all the wrong ___ to right,
sing a - long,   A Song that makes the soul feel free to be-long,
night a - way,   A Light that lights the way from day___ to day,
man - y men,   ___Lift - ing ev - 'ry bro - ken life ___ from sin,

1

Oh, I   know there is a Light,____   there is   a   Light. ___
Oh, I   (omit)
Oh, my Je - sus   is the Light,___   He   is   the Light. ___
Oh, my (omit)

2   CHORUS:

know there is a Song. ___
Je - sus   is the Song. ___   I can close ___ my eyes and still see ___ the

Light; To hear the Song I don't need a ra - di - o! ___ I can see ___

the Light changing lives ___ to - day, And I can hear the Song as o - ver and

o - ver it goes; ___ There is a Man, ___ A Man who

spreads His Light for all to see, A Man who sang His

(rit. last time)

song for lib - er - ty; Oh, my Je - sus is the Man! ___

157 I'll Meet You By The River

A. E. B.

Albert E. Brumley

1. O - ver on the bright E - ly - sian shore, Where the howling tempest comes no more,
2. Aft - er all the sor - row and the strife, Aft - er all the trou - ble of this life,
3. Aft - er all the dis - ap-point-ments here, Aft - er all the shadows dis-ap-pear,

Meet you by the riv-er some hap - py day;
I'll meet you by the riv - er some sweet day;

Far be-yond the partings and the tomb, Where the charming ros-es ev - er bloom,
When we gath-er far be - yond the sea, What a hap - py meet-ing that will be,
When the eve - ning sun at last goes down, When we go to wear a robe and crown,

Meet you by the riv - er some sweet day.
I'll meet you by the riv - er some hap-py day.

CHORUS

Meet you by the riv - er some hap-py day,
I'll meet you by the riv - er some sweet day,

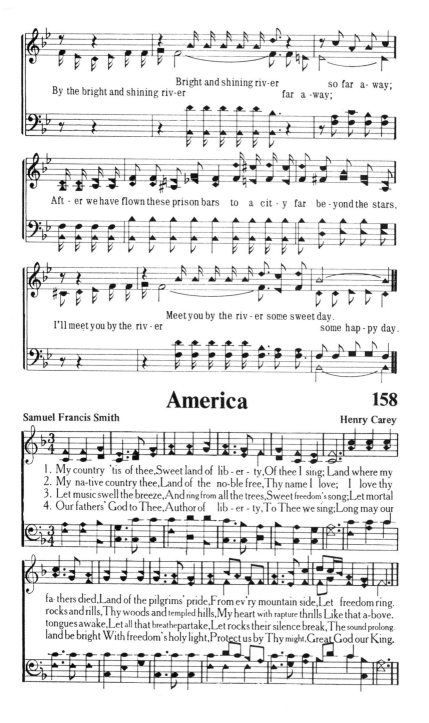

Bright and shining riv-er so far a-way;
By the bright and shining riv-er far a-way;

Aft-er we have flown these prison bars to a cit-y far be-yond the stars,

Meet you by the riv-er some sweet day.
I'll meet you by the riv-er some hap-py day.

America 158

Samuel Francis Smith   **Henry Carey**

1. My country 'tis of thee, Sweet land of lib-er-ty, Of thee I sing; Land where my
2. My na-tive country thee, Land of the no-ble free, Thy name I love; I love thy
3. Let music swell the breeze, And ring from all the trees, Sweet freedom's song; Let mortal
4. Our fathers' God to Thee, Author of lib-er-ty, To Thee we sing; Long may our

fa-thers died, Land of the pilgrims' pride, From ev'ry mountain side, Let freedom ring.
rocks and rills, Thy woods and templed hills, My heart with rapture thrills Like that a-bove.
tongues awake, Let all that breathe partake, Let rocks their silence break, The sound prolong.
land be bright With freedom's holy light, Protect us by Thy might, Great God our King.

159 I See Jesus

C.B.W.

Charles B. Wycuff

1. Once a man named Ste - phen, preached a - bout the Lord,
2. As the stones fell on him, beat - ing out his life,
3. Thro' the gates of glo - ry, down the streets of gold,

Folks were saved and folks were healed, As they heard his word;
Ste - phen knew he'd soon be thro', with all toil and strife;
Marched a he - ro of the Lord, In - to heav - ens fold;

Sa - tan did not like it, soon he had his crowd,
So much like the mas - ter, with a heart so true,
When he met the Sav - ior, at the great white throne,

And as he was tried they heard Ste - phen cry a - loud.
He prayed "Lord for - give for they know not what they do"
I be - lieve He smiled and said, "Ste - phen wel - come home"

CHORUS

"I see Je - sus, stand - ing at the Fa - ther's right hand,

I see Je - sus, yon - der in the prom - ised land;

Work is o - ver, Now I'm com - ing to thee,

I see Je - sus, stand - ing wait - ing for me."

Blest Be The Tie

160

John Fawcett

Hans G. Nageli

1. Blest be the tie that binds Our hearts in Chris - tian love;
2. Be - fore our Fa - ther's throne, We pour our ar - dent pray'rs;
3. We share our mu - tual woes, Our mu - tual bur - dens bear;
4. When we a - sun - der part, It gives us in - ward pain;

The fel - low-ship of kin - dred minds Is like to that a - bove.
Our fears, our hopes, our aims are one, Our com - forts and our cares.
And oft - en for each oth - er flows The sym - pa - thiz - ing tear.
But we shall still be joined in heart, And hope to meet a - gain.

161 Through An Empty Tomb

W. E. M.

W. Elmo Mercer

1. When I think of the cross on which my Sav - ior died A
2. Cru - el nails, bonds of death, could nev - er hold Him there; His

long time a - go for my sin,_____ I see it
love and His pow'r con - quered all!_____ Now I can

through an em - ty tomb, He's not there in - side, For the cross was not
face the storms of life, For I know He cares; He'll pro - tect, He will

CHORUS:

meant to be the end! __ For He lives! Je - sus lives! What a
guide me lest I fall. __

thrill to be - lieve! And this life is mine to share a - bun - dant-

ly; _____ Through an emp - ty tomb Cal - va - ry looks dif-f'rent, _____

Oh, yes! And it's all so ver - y pre - cious to me! _____

Jesus Loves Me

Anna B. Warner   Wm. B. Bradbury

1. Je - sus loves me! this I know, For the Bi - ble tells me so; Lit - tle
2. Je - sus loves me! He who died, Heav-en's gates to o - pen wide; He will
3. Je - sus loves me! loves me still, Tho' I'm ver - y weak and ill; From His

CHORUS

ones to Him be - long, They are weak but He is strong.
wash a - way my sin, Let His lit - tle child come in. Yes, Je - sus loves me,
shin - ing throne on high, Comes to watch me where I lie.

Yes, Je - sus loves me. Yes, Je - sus loves me, The Bi - ble tells me so.

163 Everything's Under Control

J. S.

John Stallings

1. Men's hearts __ to-day __ are fail-ing for fear; It seems that the
2. The earthquakes, the wars, and the problems of man: He holds __ them

end __ is so ver-y near; __ Our ship is lean-ing
all in the palm of His hand; I will fear no e-vil,

and the storms, they roll; __ But God __ has ev-'ry-thing __
for I'm in His fold; __ My Fa-ther has ev-'ry-thing __

CHORUS:

un-der con-trol. __ Un-der con-trol, tho' the night be
un-der con-trol. __

cold; Tho' the earth __ be shak-en and the bil-lows,

they __ may roll! I heard God whis-per to my trem-bling soul:

"Fear not, I have ev-'ry-thing __ un-der con-trol!"__

Jesus Paid It All   164

Mrs. H. M. Hall   John T. Grape

1. I hear the Sav-ior say, "Thy strength in-deed is small, Child of
2. Lord, now in-deed I find Thy pow'r, and Thine a-lone, Can
3. For noth-ing good have I Where-by Thy grace to claim — I'll
4. And when, be-fore the throne, I stand in Him com-plete, "Je-sus

Chorus

weakness watch and pray, Find in Me thine all in all."
change the lep-er's spots, And melt the heart of stone. Je-sus paid it all,
wash my garments white In the blood of Cal-v'ry's Lamb.
died my soul to save," My lips shall still re-peat.

All to Him I owe; Sin had left a crimson stain, He washed it white as snow.

165 More (Than You'll Ever Know)

P. J.

Phil Johnson

1. If I could find the right words to say to tell you just what Christ means to me, I'd say He's more than I could show, And more than you'll ever know!

2. If you could have seen me just yesterday, you'd know why He's life and He's breath to me; You'd know why He's more than I could show, And more than you'll ever know!

CHORUS:
Christ means more to me than you'll ever know; Christ means

more to me ____ than I could pos-si-bly show! ____ More,

more, ____ so much more, More than you'll ev - er know! ____

Why Not Now?

166

El Nathan

C. C. Case

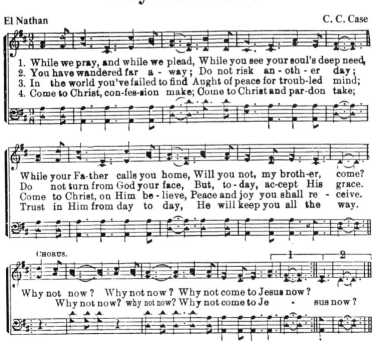

1. While we pray, and while we plead, While you see your soul's deep need,
2. You have wandered far a - way; Do not risk an - oth - er day;
3. In the world you've failed to find Aught of peace for troub-led mind;
4. Come to Christ, con-fes-sion make; Come to Christ and par-don take;

While your Fa-ther calls you home, Will you not, my broth-er, come?
Do not turn from God your face, But, to - day, ac-cept His grace.
Come to Christ, on Him be - lieve, Peace and joy you shall re - ceive.
Trust in Him from day to day, He will keep you all the way.

CHORUS.

Why not now? Why not now? Why not come to Jesus now?
Why not now? why not now? Why not come to Je - sus now?

167 Worthy The Lamb

William J. & Gloria Gaither

William J. Gaither

1. Hear the cries _____ of the shack-led from the on-set of time, For the chains _____ of de-feat there's no key; _____ See the tears of the bro-ken, the cries of the slaves, Is there no-one _____ worth-y to set us free. _____
2. Then the cry-ing _____ is _____ stilled _____ as the cho-rus rings out, The _____ shack-led re - leased from their chains; _____ And thou-sands of voic-es are swell-ing the song, _____ "Worth-y _____ the Lamb _____ that was slain." _____
3. Then all _____ the arch _____ an-gels, _____ The Saints of all time, Hold-ing their _____ crowns in their hands; _____ Fall down be-fore Him, _____ join-ing the song, _____ "Worth-y, _____ worth-y _____ the _____ Lamb." _____

CHORUS: Prayerfully

1., 2. Worth-y _____ Worth - y, _____ Worth - y the Lamb that was slain; _____
3. Bow low _____ be- fore Him, _____
4. Praise Him, _____ Praise Him, _____

Repeat to CHORUS:

Worth-y _____ Worth-y, _____
Bow low _____ be - fore Him, _____ Worth - y the Lamb that was slain. _____
Praise Him, _____ Praise Him, _____

After song is completed, other choruses may be sung using these words:

5. Love and adore Him, Worthy the Lamb that was slain.
6. Thank You, Lord Jesus, Worthy the Lamb that was slain.

Wounded For Me

168

Gladys Watkin Roberts

W. G. Ovens

1. Wound-ed for me, wound-ed for me, There on the cross
2. Dy - ing for me, dy - ing for me, There on the cross
3. Ris - en for me, ris - en for me, Up from the grave
4. Liv - ing for me, liv - ing for me, Up in the skies

He was wound - ed for me; Gone my trans - gres-sions, and
He was dy - ing for me; Now in His death my re-
He has ris - en for me; Now ev - er - more from death's
He is liv - ing for me; Dai - ly He's plead-ing and

now I am free, All be-cause Je - sus was wound-ed for me.
demp-tion I see, All be-cause Je - sus was dy - ing for me.
sting I am free, All be-cause Je - sus has ris - en for me.
pray-ing for me, All be-cause Je - sus is liv - ing for me.

169 Only One Life

L.W.

Lanny Wolfe

1. ___ It matters ___ so lit - tle ___ how much you may own, The
2. You may take ___ all the treas-ures ___ from far a - way lands, ___
3. ___The days ___ pass so swift- ly, ___ the months come and go, The

plac - es you've been ___ or the peo-ple you've known; For it all
Take all the rich - es ___ you can hold in your hands; ___ ___ And take
years melt a - way ___ ___ like new fall - en snow; ___ ___ Spring

comes to nothing ___ when placed at His feet, It's noth-ing to Je - sus,
all the pleasures ___ your mon-ey can buy, But what will you have ___
turns to summer, ___ ___ summer to fall, ___ Autumn brings winter,

CHORUS:

___ Just mem-'ries to keep. ___ On - ly one life, so soon it will
___ when it's your time to die? ___ On - ly one life, so soon it will
___ then death comes to call! ___

pass; ___ On - ly what's done for Christ will ___ last! On - ly one chance

to do His will; So give to Je-sus all your days, It's the on-ly life that pays, When you re-call you have but one life!

Almost Persuaded 170

P. P. B.

P. P. Bliss

1. "Al-most per-suad-ed" now to be-lieve; "Al-most per-suad-ed" Christ to re-ceive: Seems now some soul to say, "Go, Spir-it, go Thy way, Some more con-ven-ient day On Thee I'll call."

2. "Al-most per-suad-ed," come, come, to-day; "Al-most per-suad-ed," turn not a-way; Je-sus in-vites you here, An-gels are lin-g'ring near, Prayers rise from hearts so dear, O wan-d'rer, come.

3. "Al-most per-suad-ed," har-vest is past! "Al-most per-suad-ed," doom comes at last! "Al-most" can-not a-vail, "Al-most" is but to fail! Sad, sad, that bit-ter wail, "Al-most," but lost!

171 A Song Holy Angels Cannot Sing

G. J.

Gordon Jensen

1. An-gels nev - er knew the joy ___ that is mine, ___ For the
2. ___ "Ho-ly is the Lord," the an - gels sing, ___ ___ Be -

blood has nev - er washed their sins a - way; ___ ___ Tho' they sing in
fore the throne of God con - tin - ual - ly; ___ For me to join their

Heav - en there will come a time ___ ___ When si - lent - ly they'll
song will be a nat - 'ral thing, ___ But they just won't know the

CHORUS:

lis - ten to me sing "A - maz - ing Grace." ___ And it's a
words ___ ___ to "Love ___ Lift - ed Me." ___

song ho - ly an - gels can - not sing, ___ "A - maz - ing Grace, ___

How sweet the sound!"____ It's a song ho-ly an-gels can-not sing, ___ "I once was lost,_____ but now I'm found."____

Come, Ye Sinners

172

Joseph Hart

Anonymous

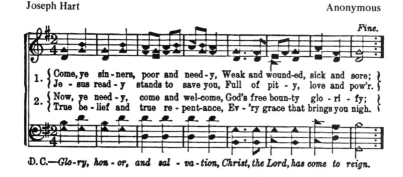

1. { Come, ye sin-ners, poor and need-y, Weak and wound-ed, sick and sore; }
{ Je-sus read-y stands to save you, Full of pit-y, love and pow'r. }

2. { Now, ye need-y, come and wel-come, God's free boun-ty glo-ri-fy; }
{ True be-lief and true re-pent-ance, Ev-'ry grace that brings you nigh. }

Fine.

D. C.—*Glo-ry, hon-or, and sal-va-tion, Christ, the Lord, has come to reign.*

CHORUS.

D. C.

Turn to the Lord and seek sal-va-tion, Sound the praise of His dear name;

3 Let not conscience make you linger,
Nor of fitness fondly dream;
All the fitness He requireth,
Is to feel your need of Him.

4 Come, ye weary, heavy-laden,
Bruised and mangled by the fall,
If you tarry till you're better,
You will never come at all.

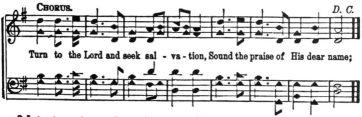

173 I'll See You In The Rapture

C. B. F.

Charles B. Feltner

1. If we nev-er meet a-gain on this earth, my pre-cious friend,
2. To my loved ones let me say that there'll sure-ly come a day,

If, to God, we have been true and we've lived a-bove all sin; Then, for
When the Lord will come a-gain and He'll take His bride a-way; So, get

us, there'll be a greet-ing, for there's gon-na be a meet-ing, I'll
read-y now to meet Him, and with hal-le-lu-jahs greet Him,

CHORUS:

see you in the rap-ture some sweet day.___ I'll see you in the

rap-ture, see you in the rap-ture, See you at that

meet-ing in the air;___ There, with our bless-ed Sav-ior, we'll

live and reign for-ev-er, I'll see you in the rap-ture some sweet day.___

Blessed Be The Name

174

Charles Wesley

R. E. Hudson

1. O for a thousand tongues to sing,
2. Je - sus! the name that charms our fears, Bless-ed be the name of the Lord!
3. He breaks the pow'r of can-celed sin,
4. I nev - er shall for-get that day,

FINE

The glo-ries of my God and King!
'Tis mu-sic in the sin-ner's ears, Bless-ed be the name of the Lord!
His blood can make the foul-est clean,
When Je-sus washed my sins a-way,

CHORUS   For 2nd ending D. S.

Bless-ed be the name, blessed be the name, Blessed be the name of the Lord!

175 Jesus, Hold My Hand

A. E. B.

Albert E. Brumley

1. As I trav-el thru this pil-grim land There is a Friend who walks with me, Leads me safe-ly thro' the sink-ing sand, It is the Christ of Cal-va-ry; This would be my pray'r, dear Lord, each day To help me do the best I can, For I need Thy light to guide me day and night Bless-ed Je-sus, hold my hand.

2. Let me trav-el in the light di-vine That I may see the bless-ed way; Keep me that I may be whol-ly Thine And sing re-demption's song some day; I will be a sol-dier brave and true And ev-er firm-ly take a stand, As I on-ward go and dai-ly meet the foe, Bless-ed Je-sus, hold my hand.

3. When I wan-der thru the val-ley dim To-ward the set-ting of the sun, Lead me safe-ly to a land of rest If I crown of life have won; I have put my faith in Thee, dear Lord, That I may reach the gold-en strand, There's no oth-er friend on whom I can de-pend, Bless-ed Je-sus, hold my hand.

CHORUS.

Je - sus, hold my hand, I need...... Thee ev-'ry
Bless-ed Je - sus, hold my hand, Yes, I need Thee

hour, Thru...... this pil - grim land Pro -
ev-'ry hour, Thru this land, this pil - grim land

tect me by Thy pow'r; Hear.... my fee-ble plea,
By Thy sav-ing pow'r; Hear my plea, my fee-ble plea,

O Lord,...... look down on me, When I kneel in
Lord, dear Lord, look down on me, When

pray'r I hope to meet you there, Bless-ed Je-sus, hold my hand.
I kneel in pray'r,

176 I Can Tell You The Time

A. M. P.

Adger M. Pace

1. I remember the time .... when in darkness I wandered, farther from home,
2. Just a sinner was I .... far a-way from my Savior, going a-lone,
3. I can nev-er for-get .... when He spoke to me gently "follow thou me"

On the mountain of sin, ... I had traveled so long, I had traveled so long;
With no hope of reward .... at the end of the way, at the end of the way;
In the fountain of life, ... there's a balm for your soul, there's a balm for your soul;

Like the prod-i-gal son, ... all my goods I had squandered, sadly I'd roam,
But the Sav-ior came down, ... and He gave me His fa-vor, all for my own,
So I heed-ed His voice, ... He was speaking intently, glad-ly I see,

But the Sav-ior came in .... and He gave me a song, 'twas a beautiful song.
Now I'm sing-ing His praise, ... for He saved me that day, truly saved me that day.
Thru His mar-vel-ous grace, ... I am happy and whole, I am happy and whole.

CHORUS

I can tell you the time,

I can tell you now, the time, I can

I can show you the place, Where the Lord saved
take you to the place,

me by His wonder-ful grace;
Where the Lord saved me by His wonder-ful grace, by His won-der-ful grace;

For I know not the how,
But I can-not tell you how, and I

and I know not the why, But He'll tell me all a-
can-not tell you why,

bout it in the by and by.
He will tell me all about it in the by and by, in the by and by.

177 If We Never Meet Again

A. E. B.

Albert E. Brumley

Slow

1. Soon we'll come to the end of life's jour-ney, And per-
2. O so oft-en we're part-ed with sor-row, Ben-e-
3. O they say we shall meet by the riv-er, Where no

haps we'll nev-er meet an-y more, Till we gath-er in
dic-tions oft-en quick-en our pain, But we nev-er shall
storm-clouds ev-er dark-en the sky, And they say we'll be

heav-en's bright cit-y Far a-way on that beau-ti-ful shore.
sor-row in heav-en, God be with you till we meet a-gain.
hap-py in heav-en In the won-der-ful sweet by and by.

CHORUS

Nev - er meet this side of heav-en
If we nev-er meet a-gain this side of heav-en

Strug-gle thru this world and its strife,
As we strug-gle thru this world and its strife, There's an-

178 One Day Too Late

L. W.

Lanny Wolfe

1. I never tho't I'd see the day when you'd come to
2. You tried to live the best you could; tried to do the

kneel and pray; I nev - er tho't that I would see
things you should; But when it came to serv - ing God,

the church house filled to ca - pa - ci - ty; ___ And out -
you said, "I still ___ have time to wait"; But now it's

side the door there's more who have nev - er come be -
all ___ turned a - round, time to serve Him now you've

fore; Oh, what a shame that Je - sus came one
found; How sad the fate: you found the time one

CHORUS:

day be - fore! _____ (1) And you came } one day too
day too late! _____ (2) You came just }

late, one day too late! Je - sus came and you've been left be -

hind to wait! _____ Yes - ter - day you could - n't find

time for Je - sus on your mind; You fin - ally came to

call His name, but one day too late! _____

179 The Spirit Of Jesus Is In This Place

William J.
& Gloria Gaither

William J. Gaither

CHORUS:

Oh, the Spir - it of Je - sus, is in this place, (in this place) I can see the change He's mak - ing on each face ___ When the pow'r of Heav'n is tapped, then, Some - thing good is bound to hap - pen, ___ for the

FINE

Spir - it of Je - sus is in this place. ___

180 Jesus Is Still The Answer

L. W.

Lanny Wolfe

1. Some — men try so hard — to — prove that God's
2. Some men pre - tend that things — of this world have bro't

not real - ly real, — While oth - ers say they know for sure
them peace of mind, — But with the dawn of each new day,

His love you can - not feel; But I know He's real with - in my soul,
new thrills they try to find; Not un - til they meet the Prince of Peace

for one day He cleansed and made me whole; and Je - sus is
can they ev - er hope to find re - lief; for Je - sus is

still — the an - swer for that long - ing deep in your soul.
still — the an - swer for a world that's seeking for peace.

CHORUS:

Je - sus is still the an - swer, and tho' time and a - ges roll, Je - sus is still ___ the an - swer, He's the an - swer for your soul; And tho' some may say He does - n't fit with their ___ phil - os - o - phy, I know Je - sus is still ___ the an - swer: He's al - ways been and al - ways will be!

181 Just A Little While

E. M. B.

E. M. Bartlett

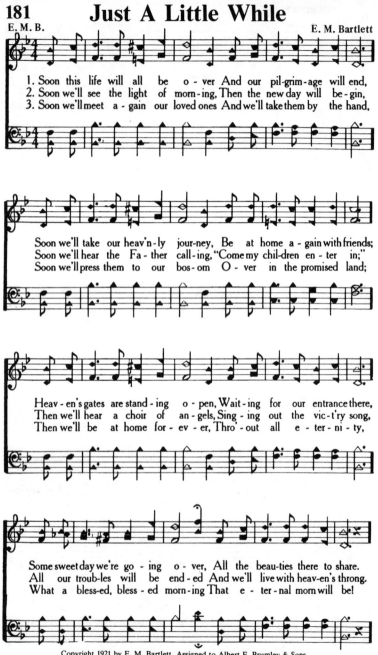

1. Soon this life will all be o-ver And our pil-grim-age will end,
2. Soon we'll see the light of morn-ing, Then the new day will be-gin,
3. Soon we'll meet a-gain our loved ones And we'll take them by the hand,

Soon we'll take our heav'n-ly jour-ney, Be at home a-gain with friends;
Soon we'll hear the Fa-ther call-ing, "Come my chil-dren en-ter in;"
Soon we'll press them to our bos-om O-ver in the promised land;

Heav-en's gates are stand-ing o-pen, Wait-ing for our entrance there,
Then we'll hear a choir of an-gels, Sing-ing out the vic-t'ry song,
Then we'll be at home for-ev-er, Thro'-out all e-ter-ni-ty,

Some sweet day we're go-ing o-ver, All the beau-ties there to share.
All our troub-les will be end-ed And we'll live with heav-en's throng.
What a bless-ed, bless-ed morn-ing That e-ter-nal morn will be!

CHORUS

Just a lit-tle while to stay here,
stay here, stay here,
Just a lit-tle while to
wait,
to wait,
Just a lit-tle while to la - bor
la - bor, la - bor,
In the path that's
al - ways straight,
that's al-ways straight and narrow
Just a lit-tle more of
trou - bles
trou - bles, trou - bles,
In this low and sin - ful state,
sin - ful state;
Then we'll en - ter heaven's por - tals,
portals, por - tals,
Sweeping thro' the pearl-y gates.
pearl-y gates.

182 I'm Free Again

V. B. E.

V. B. (Vep) Ellis

1. Sa-tan led my soul a-stray (Sa-tan led my soul a-stray I drift-ed),
2. On the sin-ful path be-low (on the sin-ful path be-low is trou-ble),
3. Soon the pearl-y gates I'll see (soon the pearl-y gates I'll see in heav-en),

From the straight and nar-row way (that leads to hap-pi-ness and life e-
All in sor-row, grief and woe, (the sin-ner's load is might-y hard to
Soon I'll live e-ter-nal-ly (And then I'll nev-er die but live for-

ter-nal); But to Je-sus I did pray, (to the Lord I hum-bly pray'd),
car-ry); But I've left the shift-ing sand, (I have left the shift-ing sand),
ev-er); Friends and loved ones wait for me, (friends and loved ones wait for me),

He heard my prayer, res-cued me that ver-y day, (that ver-y day).
Up-on the Rock, sol-id Rock, I'll take my stand, (I'll take my stand).
I'll sail up high, thru the sky, be-cause I'm free, (be-cause I'm free).

183 I Keep Falling In Love With Him

L.W.

Lanny Wolfe

1. When I first fell in love with Je - sus, _____ I gave Him all
2. There's a hand _____ that I hold on _____ to thro' each val - ley and

my heart, _____ And I thought I couldn't love Him more than I did right
each trial, _____ There's a shoulder that I lean up - on as I face an -

at the start; _____ But now I look back o - ver the moun - tains
oth - er mile; _____ _____ There's a love that I can de - pend _____ on,

and the val-leys where we've been, And it makes me know I love Him so
it's _____ fresh and new each day, _____ And with love my heart is o - ver-flow-

CHORUS:

much more than I did then! _____ And I keep fall-ing in love with Him,
ing, that is why I say: _____ _____ I keep

184 Looking For A City

W. Oliver Cooper

Marvin P. Dalton

1. Here a-mong the shad-ows (liv-ing) in a lone-ly land, With strangers
2. Here in dis-ap-pointment (oft-en) we so sad-ly roam, And earth-ly
3. In this land of dan-gers (we are) go - ing here and there We're simply

we're a band of pil-grims on the move; Thru dan-gers burdened
friends no long - er speak one word of love; But tru-ly we have
trust - ing in the bless-ed Sav-ior's love; And mer-cy tho' we

down with sor-rows, And we're shunned on ev-'ry hand, But we are look - ing
found con-tent-ment, Je-sus prom-ised us a home, So we are look - ing
may be stran-gers, Liv-ing in this world of care, We're always look - ing

CHORUS

for a cit - y built a-bove.
a-bove. O yes we're look-ing here and there

Look - -

ing for a cit - y,
Look-ing for a cit - y, Yon-der where we'll never die,

Where we'll nev-er

185 I'll Meet You In The Morning

A. E. B.

Albert E. Brumley

1. I will meet you in the morn-ing, by the bright riv-er side,
2. I will meet you in the morn-ing, in the sweet by and by,
3. I will meet you in the morn-ing, at the end of the way,

When all sor-row has drift-ed a-way; I'll be stand-ing at the
And exchange the old cross for a crown; There will be no dis-ap-
On the streets of that cit-y of gold; Where we all can be to-

por-tals, when the gates o-pen wide, At the close of life's long, dreary day.
pointments and no-bod-y shall die, In that land, when life's sun go-eth down.
geth-er and be hap-py for aye, While the years and the a-ges shall roll.

CHORUS

Meet you in the morn-ing,   meet you in the morn-ing,
I'll meet . . . . you in the morn-ing, ...

"How do you do"   "How do you do"
with a "How . . . . do you do" . . . . and we'll

sit down by the riv - er,   sit down by the riv - er,
sit down . . . . by the riv - er . . . . And with

Rap - ture   our "auld" acquaintance re-new;   Know me in the morn-
rap - ture "auld" acquaintance re - new; . . . . You'll know . . . .

ing,   know me in the morn-ing,   Smiles that I wear
me in the morn-ing, ... By the smiles . . . . that I

smiles that I wear,   Meet you in the morning,   meet you in the morning,
wear, ... When I meet you . . . . in the morning, ...

Cit - y   cit - y built, that cit - y built four square.
In the cit - y that is built,   four square . . . .

186 A Wonderful Feeling

L.W.

Lanny Wolfe

CHORUS

D.C. Well, it's a wonderful feeling when you know you've found — what you've been looking for! No more searching, no more looking a-round to find something worth liv-ing for; I found Je-sus and there's no doubt a- bout it, He's ev-'ry-thing I wanted and more, — And it's a wonderful feel-ing when you know you've found — what you've been looking for! 1. For such a long — time I 2. I did-n't know for sure just

FINE VERSE

tried — to find — just a lit - tle peace of — mind, — But
what to look for, — I did-n't know what dreams I should dream: — 'Cause

noth-ing I tried — kept — me sat-is-fied, — — no last-ing — joy — did I
ev-'ry-thing that glitters and looks so bright is-n't al-ways _____ as it

find: But when I found Je - sus some-thing deep in - side — me
seems: Just when I thought hap - pi - ness _____ could-n't be found, —

said "Your searching — is fin - al-ly o'er": And it's a wonderful feel-
— The Sav - ior — knocked at my door, And it's a wonderful feel-

D.C.

- ing when you know you've found — what you've been — looking for!
- ing when you know you've found — what you've been — looking for!

187 Build My Mansion

D. R.

Dottie Rambo

1. I have no cas-tles no earth-ly king-dom, But my
2. My moth-er's man-sion may be close by me, A-

cab-in will do 'til I get home; My man-sion's
cross the gold-en av-e-nue; She was the

yon-der on the hills of glo-ry, Oh I hope my
first one to teach me of heav-en, And the ver-y

CHORUS

man-sion sits near God's throne. Build my man-sion
first one Lord to tell me about you. Build my man-sion

next door to Je-sus, And tell the an-gels I'm com-ing

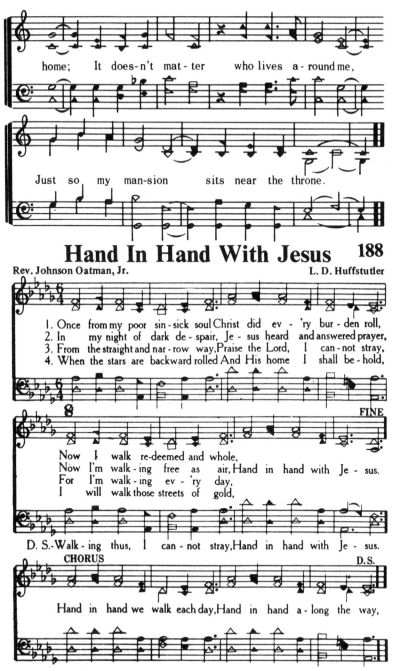

home; It does-n't mat-ter who lives a-round me,

Just so my man-sion sits near the throne.

Hand In Hand With Jesus 188

Rev. Johnson Oatman, Jr.

L. D. Huffstutler

1. Once from my poor sin-sick soul Christ did ev-'ry bur-den roll,
2. In my night of dark de-spair, Je-sus heard and answered prayer,
3. From the straight and nar-row way, Praise the Lord, I can-not stray,
4. When the stars are backward rolled And His home I shall be-hold,

FINE

Now I walk re-deemed and whole,
Now I'm walk-ing free as air, Hand in hand with Je-sus.
For I'm walk-ing ev-'ry day,
I will walk those streets of gold,

D. S.-Walk-ing thus, I can-not stray, Hand in hand with Je-sus.

CHORUS

D.S.

Hand in hand we walk each day, Hand in hand a-long the way,

189 That Day Is Almost Here

L. T.

LaVerne Tripp

1. For so long now we've dreamed a-bout that day that soon shall come, When He would split the eastern skies and gath - er all His jew - els home; I've gone too far to turn back now, at last the vic - t'ry's al - most won, I've fought the fight, I've kept the faith, thank God, I'm al - most home.

2. You ask me how I know it's real, these things I just can't ex - plain, For all I know is that heav - en - ly tug I can feel on my heart strings; It won't be long, and I will see old Jor - dan break-ing at my feet, Then up a - head, the lights of home, it's o - ver, my jour - ney's now com - plete.

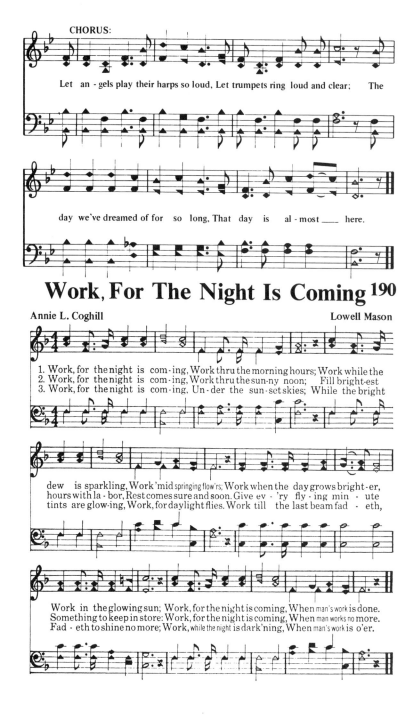

CHORUS:

Let an-gels play their harps so loud, Let trumpets ring loud and clear; The

day we've dreamed of for so long, That day is al-most ___ here.

Work, For The Night Is Coming 190

Annie L. Coghill

Lowell Mason

1. Work, for the night is com-ing, Work thru the morning hours; Work while the
2. Work, for the night is com-ing, Work thru the sun-ny noon; Fill bright-est
3. Work, for the night is com-ing, Un-der the sun-set skies; While the bright

dew is sparkling, Work 'mid springing flow'rs; Work when the day grows bright-er,
hours with la-bor, Rest comes sure and soon. Give ev-'ry fly-ing min-ute
tints are glow-ing, Work, for daylight flies. Work till the last beam fad-eth,

Work in the glowing sun; Work, for the night is coming, When man's work is done.
Something to keep in store: Work, for the night is coming, When man works no more.
Fad-eth to shine no more; Work, while the night is dark'ning, When man's work is o'er.

191 What A Day That Will Be

J. H.

Jim Hill

1. There is com-ing a day when no heart - aches shall come, No more
2. There'll be no sor-row there, no more bur - dens to bear, No more

clouds in the sky, no more tears to dim the eye; All is peace
sick - ness, no pain, no more part - ing o - ver there; And for - ev -

for - ev - er-more on that hap - py gold - en shore, What a day glo - ri - ous
er I will be with the One who died for me,

CHORUS

day that will be. What a day that will be when my Je - sus

I shall see, And I look up - on His face, the One who saved me

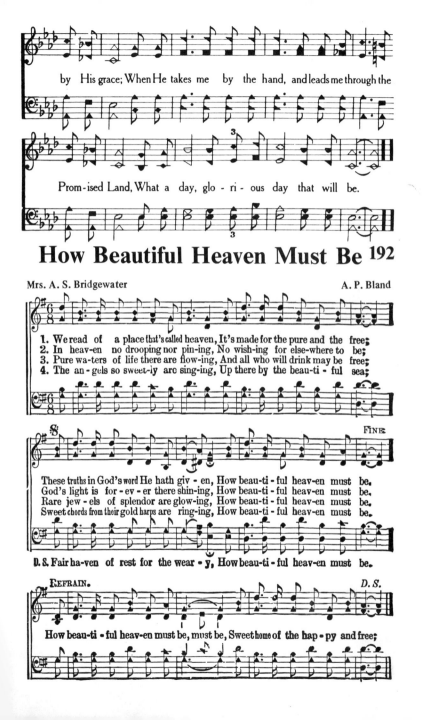

by His grace; When He takes me by the hand, and leads me through the

Prom-ised Land, What a day, glo-ri-ous day that will be.

How Beautiful Heaven Must Be 192

Mrs. A. S. Bridgewater

A. P. Bland

1. We read of a place that's called heaven, It's made for the pure and the free;
2. In heav-en no drooping nor pin-ing, No wish-ing for else-where to be;
3. Pure wa-ters of life there are flow-ing, And all who will drink may be free;
4. The an-gels so sweet-ly are sing-ing, Up there by the beau-ti-ful sea;

These truths in God's word He hath giv-en, How beau-ti-ful heav-en must be.
God's light is for-ev-er there shin-ing, How beau-ti-ful heav-en must be.
Rare jew-els of splendor are glow-ing, How beau-ti-ful heav-en must be.
Sweet chords from their gold harps are ring-ing, How beau-ti-ful heav-en must be.

D. S. Fair ha-ven of rest for the wear-y, How beau-ti-ful heav-en must be.

REFRAIN.

D. S.

How beau-ti-ful heav-en must be, must be, Sweet home of the hap-py and free;

193
I Love Him Too Much
(To Fail Him Now)

L.W.

Lanny Wolfe

1. When I first heard ___ of Je - sus, ___ His love ___ and ___ His grace,
2. I ___ told Him ___ I loved Him, It was eas - y ___ to say,
3. Oh, the years have drawn us clo-ser, ___ My love for Him ___ has grown;

My heart was o - verwhelmed ___ to think a king would take my place! ___
But hard - er to prove it ___ when temp-ta - tion came my way; ___
Each step has bro't me near - er ___ to my e - ter - nal home; And

I cried, "Lord, ___ I'll go with you ___ ev - 'ry step of ___ the way;
For what good ___ are bro - ken promis - es, ___ I count-ed them but loss
I'm just too close ___ to Heav - en ___ to turn ___ back now,

___ That's all ___ I can do, ___ my debt to ___ re - pay."
When I caught a glimpse of true love ___ hang-ing on ___ a rug - ged cross!
___ His grace will be suf - fic - ient, I'm gon-na make it ___ somehow!

CHORUS:

I love Him too much to fail ___ Him now! Too much to break ___ my

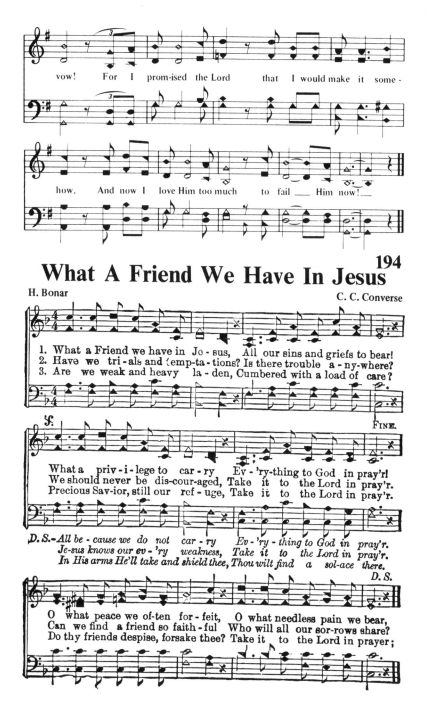

vow! For I prom-ised the Lord that I would make it some-

how, And now I love Him too much to fail ___ Him now!

What A Friend We Have In Jesus

194

H. Bonar

C. C. Converse

1. What a Friend we have in Je-sus, All our sins and griefs to bear!
2. Have we tri-als and temp-ta-tions? Is there trouble a-ny-where?
3. Are we weak and heavy la-den, Cumbered with a load of care?

FINE.

What a priv-i-lege to car-ry Ev-'ry-thing to God in pray'r!
We should never be dis-cour-aged, Take it to the Lord in pray'r.
Precious Sav-ior, still our ref-uge, Take it to the Lord in pray'r.

D. S.—All be-cause we do not car-feit, Ev-'ry-thing to God in pray'r.
Je-sus knows our ev-'ry weakness, Take it to the Lord in pray'r.
In His arms He'll take and shield thee, Thou wilt find a sol-ace there.

D. S.

O what peace we of-ten for-feit, O what needless pain we bear,
Can we find a friend so faith-ful Who will all our sor-rows share?
Do thy friends despise, forsake thee? Take it to the Lord in prayer;

195 Nailing My Sins To His Cross

W. E. M.

W. Elmo Mercer

1. That day when they cru-ci-fied my Sav-ior ____ He was
2. Al-though this was cen-tur-ies a-go now ____ And I

will-ing ____ to pay ____ all the cost ____ When they drove
was-n't e-ven liv-ing then at all ____ The Bi-ble

nails. cru-el nails through His bod-y ____ They were nail-ing
says Je-sus died for all sin-ners ____ This in-cludes me

CHORUS

my sins to His cross ____ O. the shame of it! My sins
O praise His dear name! ____

cru-ci-fied Him that day! My sins were to blame ____ For-give.

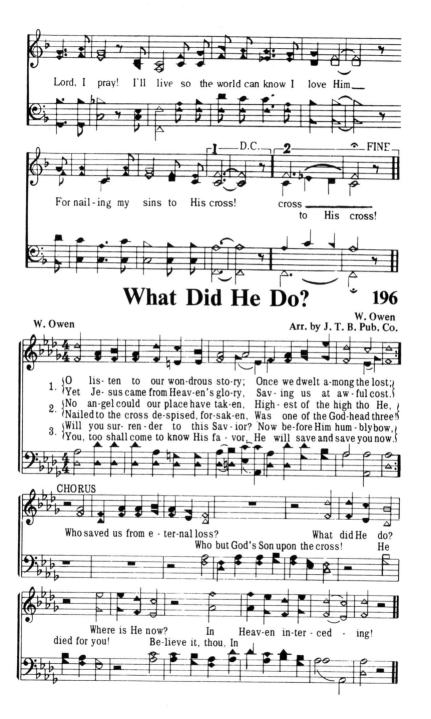

Lord, I pray! I'll live so the world can know I love Him

For nail-ing my sins to His cross!   cross   to His cross!

[1 — D.C.] [2 — FINE]

What Did He Do?   196

W. Owen

W. Owen
Arr. by J. T. B. Pub. Co.

1. {O lis-ten to our won-drous sto-ry; Once we dwelt a-mong the lost;
   {Yet Je-sus came from Heav-en's glo-ry, Sav-ing us at aw-ful cost.}

2. {No an-gel could our place have tak-en, High-est of the high tho He,
   {Nailed to the cross de-spised, for-sak-en, Was one of the God-head three!}

3. {Will you sur-ren-der to this Sav-ior? Now be-fore Him hum-bly bow,
   {You, too shall come to know His fa-vor, He will save and save you now.}

CHORUS

Who saved us from e-ter-nal loss?   What did He do?
Who but God's Son upon the cross!   He

Where is He now?   In Heav-en in-ter-ced - ing!
died for you!   Be-lieve it, thou. In

197 Just A Little Talk With Jesus

Spiritual

Cleavant Derricks

1. I once was lost in sin but Je-sus took me in, And then a lit-tle
2. Some-times my path seems drear, with-out a ray of cheer, And then a cloud of
3. I may have doubts and fears, my eyes be filled with tears, But Je-sus is a

light from heav-en filled my soul; It bathed my heart in love and wrote my
doubt may hide the light of day; The mists of sin may rise and hide the
Friend Who watches day and night; I go to Him in prayer, He knows my

name a-bove, And just a lit-tle talk with Je-sus made me whole.
star-ry skies, But just a lit-tle talk with Je-sus clears the way.
ev-'ry care, And just a lit-tle talk with Je-sus makes it right.

CHORUS

Have a lit-tle talk with Je-sus, tell Him all a-bout our
Now let us   let us

trou-bles,   Hear our faint-est cry   an-swer by and by;
He will   and He will

Now when you Feel a lit-tle prayer wheel turn-ing
Then you'll know a lit-tle fire is

You will burn-ing, Find a lit-tle talk with Je-sus makes it right.
it makes it right.

Cleanse Me
198

J. Edwin Orr

Maori Melody
Arr. by John T. Benson, Jr.

1. Search me, O God, and know my heart to-day; Try me, O
2. I praise Thee, Lord, for cleans-ing me from sin; Ful-fill Thy
3. Lord, take my life, and make it whol-ly Thine; Fill my poor
4. O Ho-ly Ghost, re-viv-al comes from Thee; Send a re-

Sav-ior, know my tho'ts, I pray: See if there be some wick-ed
Word, and make me pure with-in; Fill me with fire, where once I
heart with Thy great love di-vine; Take all my will, my pas-sion,
viv-al, start the work in me: Thy Word de-clares Thou wilt sup-

way in me: Cleanse me from ev-'ry sin, and set me free.
burned with shame: Grant my de-sire to mag-ni-fy Thy name.
self and pride; I now sur-ren-der:Lord, in me a-bide.
ply our need: For bless-ing now, O Lord, I hum-bly plead.

199 Jesus Is Coming Soon

R. E. W.

R. E. Winsett

1. Trou-ble-some times are here, fill-ing men's hearts with fear,
2. Love of so man - y cold, los-ing their homes of gold,
3. Trou-bles will soon be o'er, hap-py for ev - er-more,

Free-dom we all hold dear now is at stake; Humb'ling your
This in God's Word is told, e - vil's a-bound; When these signs
When we meet on that shore, free from all care; Ris - ing up

heart to God, saves from the chast-'ning rod, Seek the way
come to pass, near-ing the end at last, It will come
in the sky, tell-ing this world good- bye, Homeward we

Fine   *Refrain*

pil - grims trod, Christians a- wake.__ Je - sus is com - ing
ver - y fast, trumpets will sound.__ Je - sus is com-ing
then will fly, glo - ry to share.__

D.S. Heav - en - ward bound.

soon, morning or night or noon, Many will meet their
soon, morning or night or noon, Man-y will meet their

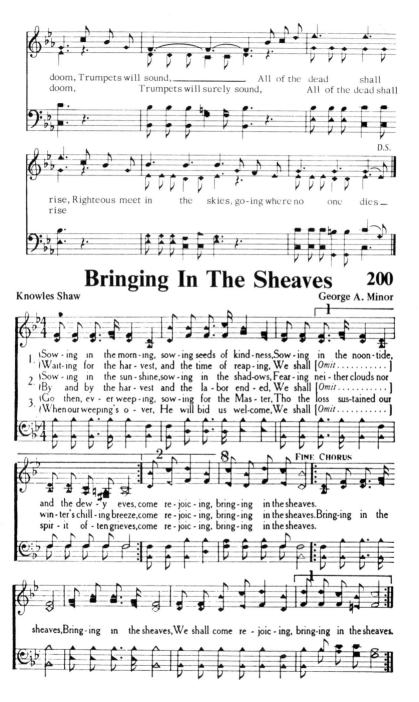

doom, Trumpets will sound,_____ All of the dead shall
doom, Trumpets will surely sound, All of the dead shall

D.S.

rise, Righteous meet in the skies, go-ing where no one dies_
rise

Bringing In The Sheaves 200

Knowles Shaw   George A. Minor

1. Sow-ing in the morn-ing, sow-ing seeds of kind-ness,Sow-ing in the noon-tide.
   Wait-ing for the har-vest, and the time of reap-ing, We shall [Omit..........]
2. Sow-ing in the sun-shine,sow-ing in the shad-ows,Fear-ing nei-ther clouds nor
   By and by the har-vest and the la-bor end-ed, We shall [Omit..........]
3. Go then, ev-er weep-ing, sow-ing for the Mas-ter,Tho the loss sus-tained our
   When our weeping's o-ver, He will bid us wel-come,We shall [Omit..........]

FINE CHORUS

and the dew-y eves, come re-joic-ing, bring-ing in the sheaves.
win-ter's chill-ing breeze,come re-joic-ing, bring-ing in the sheaves.Bring-ing in the
spir-it of-ten grieves,come re-joic-ing, bring-ing in the sheaves.

sheaves,Bring-ing in the sheaves,We shall come re-joic-ing, bring-ing in the sheaves.

201 Remind Me, Dear Lord

D. R.

Dottie Rambo

1. The __ things that I love and hold dear to my heart Are just
2. Noth-ing good have I done to de-serve God's own Son; I'm not

bor-rowed __ they're not mine at all __ Je-sus on-ly let me
wor-thy of the scars in His hands __ Yet He chose the road to

use them to brighten my life, So re-mind me, re-mind me, dear Lord. __
Cal-v'ry to die in my stead; Why He loved me, I can't un-der-stand. __

CHORUS

Roll back the cur-tain of mem-'ry now and then;

Show me where you brought me from, and where I could have been;

Re - mem - ber I'm hu - man, and hu - mans for - get;

So re - mind me, re - mind me, dear Lord. ____

Precious Memories

202

J. B. F. W.

J. B. F. Wright

1. Precious mem-'ries, un-seen an-gels, Sent from somewhere to my soul;
2. Precious fa - ther, lov-ing moth-er, Fly a - cross the lone-ly years;
3. As I trav - el on life's pathway, Know not what the years may hold;

FINE

How they lin - ger, ev - er near me, And the sa - cred past un - fold.
And old home scenes of my childhood, In fond mem-o - ry ap-pear.
As I pon - der, hope grows fond - er, Pre-cious mem-'ries flood my soul.

D. S.-In the still-ness of the midnight, Pre-cious, sa - cred scenes un - fold.

CHORUS

D.S.

Precious mem-'ries, how they lin - ger, How they ev - er flood my soul;

203 We're Not Strangers Anymore

D. L.

Danny Lee

1. From a man-ger where He lay___ to the gar-den where
2. I had heard a-bout this Man ___ who could e - ven raise
3. If you're looking for a friend ___ who'll go with you to

He prayed, ___ I'd oft-en heard a-bout this Stran - ger;
the dead, ___ I heard He calmed the troubled wa - ters;
the end, ___ Someone who's closer than a broth - er; ___

But then I o-pened up my heart ___ ___ and He walked in -
___ But I nev-er tho't for me ___ ___ He would calm the
___ Why not give this Man a try, ___ for e - ven now He's

to my life, ___ Now we're not stran-gers an - y - more.
rag - ing sea, ___ But all I do is call ___ His name.
pass - ing by, ___ You won't be stran-gers an - y - more.

CHORUS:

(1 & 2) For He's my Friend, He's my Lord, ___ Oh, how I
(3) He'll be your Friend, and your Lord, ___ Oh, how you'll

love Him, He's my Fa - ther; _____ Now we walk __
love Him, as your Fa - ther; _____ Then you'll walk __

hand in hand, __ For we're not stran-gers an - y - more. __
hand in hand, __ You won't be stran-gers an - y - more. __

204

Leaning On The Everlasting Arms

E. A. Hoffman
A. J. Showalter

1 { What a fel - low-ship, what a joy di - vine, Lean-ing on the ev - er -
  { What a bless - ed-ness, what a peace is mine, Lean-ing on the ev - er -
2 { O how sweet to walk in this pil-grim way, Lean-ing on the ev - er -
  { O how bright the path grows from day to day, Lean-ing on the ev - er -
3 { What have I to dread, what have I to fear, Lean-ing on the ev - er -
  { I have bless- ed peace with my Lord so near, Lean-ing on the ev - er -

last - ing arms;   Lean - - ing, lean - - ing,
last - - - ing arms. Lean-ing on Je - sus, lean-ing on Je - sus,

Chorus

Safe and se-cure from all a-larms;
(Omit.........................) Leaning on the ev - er - last-ing arms,

205 Come And Dine

C. C. Widmeyer

S. H. Bolton

1. Je - sus has a ta - ble spread Where the saints of God are fed,
2. The dis - ci - ples came to land, Thus o - bey - ing Christ's command,
3. Soon the Lamb will take His bride To be ev - er at His side,

He in - vites His chos - en peo - ple "Come and dine;" With His man - na
For the Mas - ter called un - to them "Come and dine;" There they found their
All the host of heav - en will as - sem - bled be; O, 'twill be a

He doth feed And sup-plies our ev - 'ry need; O 'tis sweet to sup with
hearts' de - sire, Bread and fish up - on the fire; Thus He sat - is - fies the
glo - rious sight, All the saints in spot-less white; And with Je - sus they will

CHORUS

Je - sus all the time! "Come and, dine," the Mas - ter call - eth, "Come and
hun - gry ev - 'ry time.
feast e - ter - nal - ly.

dine;" You may feast at Je - sus' ta - ble all the
O come and dine;

time; He who fed the mul-ti-tude, Turned the
O come and dine;
wa-ter in-to wine, To the hun-gry call-eth now, "Come and dine."

My Faith Looks Up To Thee 206

Ray Palmer

Lowell Maso,

1. My faith looks up to Thee, Thou Lamb of Cal-va-ry,
2. May Thy rich grace im-part Strength to my faint-ing heart,
3. While life's dark maze I tread, And griefs a-round me spread,
4. When ends life's tran-sient dream, When death's cold, sul-len stream

Sav-ior di-vine! Now hear me while I pray, Take all my
My zeal in-spire; As Thou hast died for me, O may my
Be Thou my Guide; Bid dark-ness turn to day, Wipe sor-row's
Shall o're me roll; Blest Sav-ior, then, in love, Fear and dis-

guilt a-way, O let me from this day Be whol-ly Thine!
love to Thee Pure, warm, and changeless be, A liv-ing fire!
tears a-way, Nor let me ev-er stray From Thee a-side.
trust re-move; O bear me safe a-bove, A ran-somed soul!

207 Broken Pieces

Ruby Kitchen & James Martin, Jr.

Ruby Kitchen

1. Have you failed in life's bat-tle To ac-complish __ your plans? Is
2. You may feel that there's no hope Broken hearts __ just cannot mend; Tho'

your heart __ heav-y la-den? Do you fear the Lord's command? Do you
you're torn in man-y piec-es, Christ can make you whole again; Storms of

feel that no one loves you And there's no use to try? Just bring your cares
doubt blow all di-rections, But don't you be afraid. God can make all

CHORUS

to Je-sus, __ Your __ soul He'll sat-is-fy. Pick up the bro-ken
cor-rections, He made a bod-y out of clay!

piec-es And bring them to the Lord; Pick up the broken piec-es, Trust

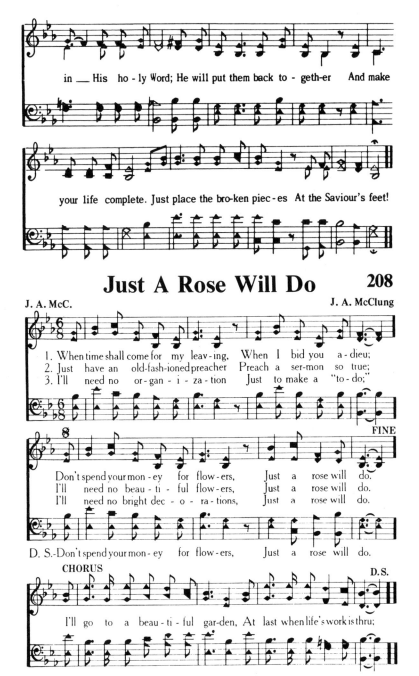

in __ His ho - ly Word; He will put them back to - geth-er And make

your life complete. Just place the bro-ken piec-es At the Saviour's feet!

Just A Rose Will Do

208

J. A. McC.

J. A. McClung

1. When time shall come for my leav-ing, When I bid you a-dieu;
2. Just have an old-fash-ioned preacher Preach a ser-mon so true;
3. I'll need no or-gan-i-za-tion Just to make a "to-do;"

FINE

Don't spend your mon-ey for flow-ers, Just a rose will do.
I'll need no beau-ti-ful flow-ers, Just a rose will do.
I'll need no bright dec-o-ra-tions, Just a rose will do.

D. S.-Don't spend your mon-ey for flow-ers, Just a rose will do.

CHORUS

D.S.

I'll go to a beau-ti-ful gar-den, At last when life's work is thru;

Arr. © 1948 by The Hartford Music Co., owners of original in "Golden Gates".

209 In The Garden

C. A. M.

C. Austin Miles

1. I come to the gar-den a-lone, While the dew is still on the
2. He speaks,and the sound of His voice Is so sweet the birds hush their
3. I'd stay in the gar-den with Him Tho' the night a-round me be

ros - es; And the voice I hear, Fall-ing on my ear; The
sing - ing, And the mel-o-dy That He gave to me, With-
fall - ing, But He bids me go; Thro' the voice of woe, His

Son of God dis - clos - es.
in my heart is ring - ing.
voice to me is call - ing.

CHORUS.

And He walks with me, and He

talks with me, And He tells me I am His own, And the

joy we share as we tar - ry there, None oth-er has ev - er known.

The Blood That Stained
The Old Rugged Cross

210

A. E. B.   *Very slow*   Albert E. Brumley

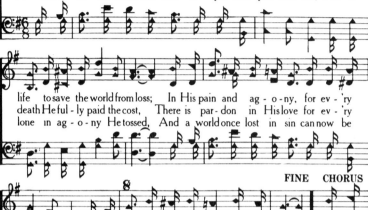

1. On the cross of Cal-va-ry our bless-ed Sav-ior died, Gave His
2. To the cross, the rug-ged cross they nailed His pre-cious hands And in
3. What an aw-ful death He died to par-don you and me, All a-

life to save the world from loss; In His pain and ag-o-ny, for ev-'ry
death He ful-ly paid the cost, There is par-don in His love for ev-'ry
lone in ag-o-ny He tossed, And a world once lost in sin can now be

FINE   **CHORUS**

sin to hide, Shed the
one that stands For the blood that stained the old rug-ged cross. 'Twas His
whol-ly free By the

blood, His precious blood that stained the old rug-ged cross, 'Twas His love that paid the

D.S.

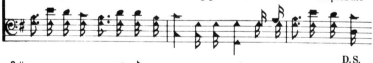

aw-ful cost; O soul so far a-stray come and plunge today In the

211 He Cared That Much For Me

W. E. M.

W. Elmo Mercer

1. When I think of Je - sus love, And how He came from heav'n a - bove, I'm a-shamed be - cause I know That I have failed my thanks to show.

2. Load I pray for strength to - day That I may show some soul the way. Af - ter all You've done for me, Can I give less than all to Thee.

CHORUS

I know, I know He loved me, This He proved at Cal - va - ry. He gave His life that I might live; He cared that much for me.

Joy Unspeakable

212

B. E. W.

Lively.

B. E. Warren

1. I have found His grace is all complete, He sup-pli-eth ev-'ry need;
2. I have found the pleasure I once craved, It is joy and peace with-in;
3. I have found that hope so bright and clear, Liv-ing in the realm of grace;
4. I have found the joy no tongue can tell, How its waves of glo-ry roll!

While I sit and learn at Je-sus' feet, I am free, yes, free in-deed....
What a wondrous blessing! I am saved From the aw-ful gulf of sin....
Oh, the Saviour's presence is so near, I can see His smil-ing face....
It is like a great o'er-flow-ing well, Springing up with-in my soul....

CHORUS.

It is joy un-speak-a-ble and full of glo-ry, Full of glo-ry, full of glo-ry; It is joy un-speak-a-ble and full of glo-ry, Oh, the half has nev-er yet been told.

213 Supper Time

I. F. S.

Ira F. Stanphill

Duet Soprano (or Tenor) and Alto.

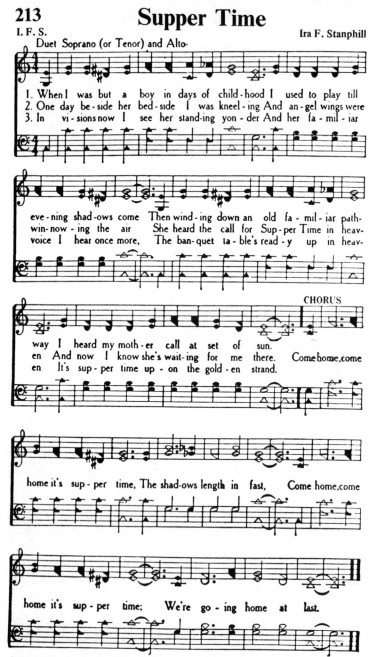

1. When I was but a boy in days of child-hood I used to play till eve-ning shad-ows come Then wind-ing down an old fa-mil-iar path-way I heard my moth-er call at set of sun.
2. One day be-side her bed-side I was kneel-ing And an-gel wings were win-now-ing the air She heard the call for Sup-per Time in heav-en And now I know she's wait-ing for me there.
3. In vi-sions now I see her stand-ing yon-der And her fa-mil-iar voice I hear once more, The ban-quet ta-ble's read-y up in heav-en It's sup-per time up-on the gold-en strand.

CHORUS

Come home, come home it's sup-per time, The shad-ows length-in fast, Come home, come home it's sup-per time; We're go-ing home at last.

Blessed Redeemer

214

Avis Burgeson Christiansen

1. Up Cal-vary's mountain one dreadful morn, Walked Christ my Saviour, weary and worn;
2. "Fa-ther, forgive them!" thus did He pray, E'en while His life-blood flowed fast a-way;
3. O how I love Him, Sav-iour and Friend, How can my prais-es ev - er find end!

Fac-ing for sin-ners death on the cross, That He might save them from endless loss.
Pray-ing for sin-ners while in such woe— No one but Je - sus ev - er loved so.
Thro' years un-num-bered on heaven's shore, My tongue shall praise Him for-ev-er-more.

CHORUS

Bless-ed Re-deem - er! pre-cious Re-deem - er! Seems now I
Bless-ed Re-deem-er! bless-ed Re-deem - er!

see Him on Cal-va-ry's tree; Wound-ed and bleed - ing, for sin-ners
Wound-ed and bleed-ing,

plead - ing— Blind and un-heed - - ing— dy-ing for me!
for sin-ners plead-ing— Blind and un-heed - ing—

Tears Are A Language

215

(God Understands)

G. J.

Gordon Jensen

1. Oft - en you've won-dered why___ tears come in - to your eyes,___
2. When grief has left you low,___ it caus-es tears to flow,___

And bur - dens seem to be much more than you can stand, ___
___ Things have not turned out the way that you had planned, ___

But God is___ stand-ing near,___ He sees your fall-ing tears,___
But God won't for- get ___ you,___ His prom-is - es are true,___

CHORUS

Tears are_ a lan - guage God un-der-stands.___ God sees the
Tears are_ a lan - guage God un-der-stands.___

tears of a brok-en heart-ed soul, ___ He sees your tears and
soul, ___

hears them when they fall;___ God weeps a - long with man, And takes him

by the hand;___ Tears are___ a lan - guage God un - der - stands.___

Did You Think To Pray? 216

Mrs. M. A. Kidder

W. O Perkins

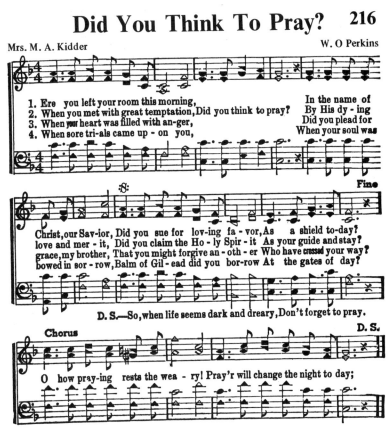

1. Ere you left your room this morning,
2. When you met with great temptation, Did you think to pray?
3. When your heart was filled with an-ger,
4. When sore tri-als came up - on you,

In the name of
By His dy - ing
Did you plead for
When your soul was

Christ, our Sav-ior, Did you sue for lov-ing fa - vor, As a shield to-day?
love and mer - it, Did you claim the Ho - ly Spir - it As your guide and stay?
grace, my brother, That you might forgive an - oth - er Who have crossed your way?
bowed in sor - row, Balm of Gil - ead did you bor-row At the gates of day?

D. S.—So, when life seems dark and dreary, Don't forget to pray.

Chorus

D. S.

O how pray-ing rests the wea - ry! Pray'r will change the night to day;

217 Don't Take My Cross Away

D. R.

Dottie Rambo

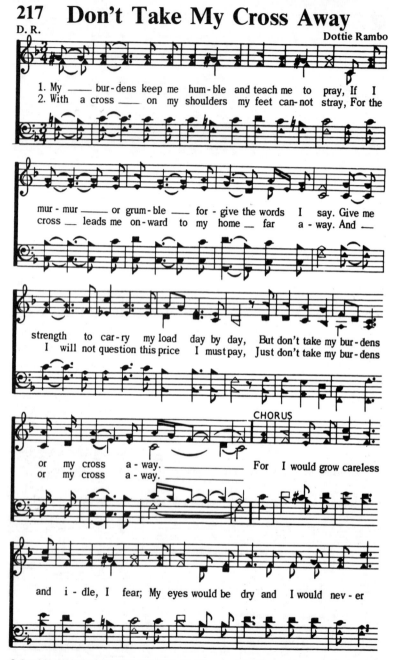

1. My _____ bur-dens keep me hum-ble and teach me to pray, If I
2. With a cross _____ on my shoulders my feet can-not stray, For the

mur-mur _____ or grum-ble _____ for-give the words I say. Give me
cross _____ leads me on-ward to my home _____ far a-way. And _____

strength to car-ry my load day by day, But don't take my bur-dens
I will not question this price I must pay, Just don't take my bur-dens

CHORUS

or my cross a-way. _____ For I would grow careless
or my cross a-way. _____

and i-dle, I fear; My eyes would be dry and I would nev-er

shed a tear ___ Lest I for-get that I need you each day,

Don't take my bur - dens or my cross a - way. ___

I'll Be True, Precious Jesus 218

Arranged Elizabeth Pate

1. I'll be true pre-cious Je-sus, I'll be true, I'll be true pre-cious
2. I'll go thru pre-cious Je-sus, I'll go thru, I'll go thru pre-cious

Je-sus, I'll be true; There's a race to be run, There's a
Je-sus, I'll go thru;

vic-t'ry to be won ev-'ry hour, by Thy pow-er I'll be true.

219 This Could Be The Dawning Of That Day

William J. & Gloria Gaither

William J. Gaither

1. A parade ___ began at Cal-v'ry, ___ ___ The saints of all the ages fill it's ranks; ___ O'er the sands of time they're marching to their King's great cor-o-na-tion, And this could be the dawn-ing of that ___ day! ___

2. Noth-ing here ___ holds their al-le-giance, ___ They're not bound by shack-les forged of earth-ly gold; ___ Since that day they knelt at Cal-v'ry, they've been pil-grims e-ver wan-d'ring, Just look-ing for a place to rest their ___ souls. ___

3. All the saints ___ are get-ting rest-less, ___ Oh, what glo-rious ex-pec-ta-tion fills each face! ___ Dreams and hopes of all the a-ges are a-wait-ing His re-turn-ing, And this could be the dawn-ing of that ___ day! ___

CHORUS:

Oh, this could be the dawn-ing of that grand and glo-rious day, When the face of Je-sus we be-hold! ___

Dreams and hopes of all the a - ges are a - wait - ing His re - turn - ing,

1-2   D. C.   3   FINE

And this could be the dawn - ing of that day! _____   day! _____

Jesus, Savior, Pilot Me   **220**

Edward Hopper

J. E. Gould

1. Je - sus, Sav - ior, pi - lot me O - ver life's tem - pes - tuous sea:
2. As a moth - er stills her child, Thou canst hush the o - cean wild;
3. When at last I near the shore, And the fear - ful break - ers roar

Un-known waves be - fore me roll, Hid - ing rocks and treacherous shoal;
Bois-terous waves o - bey Thy will When Thou sayest to them, "Be still!"
'Twixt me and the peace-ful rest, Then, while lean - ing on Thy breast,

Chart and com - pass come from Thee, Je - sus, Sav - ior, pi - lot me.
Won-drous Sov-ereign of the sea, Je - sus, Sav - ior, pi - lot me.
May I hear Thee say to me, "Fear not, I will pi - lot thee."

221 Thank You For The Valley

D. R.

Dottie Rambo

1. _ Thank You for the val-ley I_ walked thro' to-day; The
2. Life can't be all_ sun-shine or the flow-ers would die; The

dark-er the_ val-ley the more I learn to pray; _ I
riv-ers would be des-ert, all bar - ren and dry; Life_

found You where the li - ly's_ _____ bloom-ing by the way;
can't be all _____ bless-ing_ or there'd be no need to pray;

And I thank You for the val-ley I walked_ thro'_ to-day.
So I thank You for the val-ley I walked_ thro'_ to-day.

CHORUS

Thank You for ev-'ry hill I climbed, For ev-'ry time the sun did-n't shine;

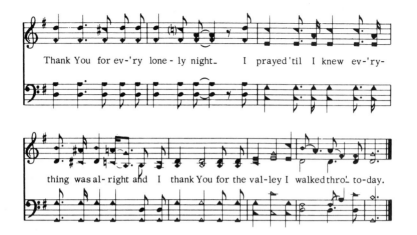

Thank You for ev-'ry lone-ly night_ I prayed 'til I knew ev-'ry-

thing was al-right and I thank You for the val-ley I walked thro' to-day.

Rock Of Ages

222

Augustus M. Toplady

Thomas Hastings

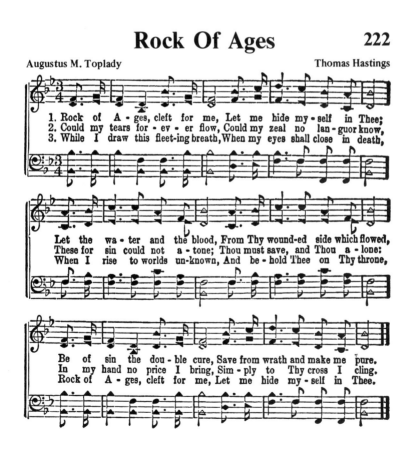

1. Rock of A - ges, cleft for me, Let me hide my - self in Thee;
2. Could my tears for - ev - er flow, Could my zeal no lan - guor know,
3. While I draw this fleet-ing breath, When my eyes shall close in death,

Let the wa - ter and the blood, From Thy wound-ed side which flowed,
These for sin could not a - tone; Thou must save, and Thou a - lone:
When I rise to worlds un-known, And be - hold Thee on Thy throne,

Be of sin the dou - ble cure, Save from wrath and make me pure.
In my hand no price I bring, Sim - ply to Thy cross I cling.
Rock of A - ges, cleft for me, Let me hide my - self in Thee.

223 Before He Calls Again

G. J.

Gordon Jensen

1. How man-y times has the Sav-ior called be-fore? And each time
2. Storm clouds are dark-en-ing your skies, The pain of

you turned a - way from His door! You said, "Not this time,
life with tears has filled your eyes; Years of sor-row

Oh! but some-day I'll get in." Tho' your lit-tle world may
you might have saved, my friend, If on - ly you had

CHORUS

crum-ble be-fore He calls a - gain. Be-fore the Sav- ior calls a-
an - swered when He called back then.

gain, You may cry a mil-lion tears; Be-fore He calls a-gain You may

waste pre-cious years! He's call-ing now, the door is o-pen, Come in-side

while you can! You may suf-fer—needless heartache before He calls a-gain!

Near The Cross

224

Fanny J. Crosby

W. H. Doane

1. Je - sus, keep me near the cross, There a pre-cious fountain, Free to all, a
2. Near the cross, a trembling soul, Love and mer - cy found me; There the Bright and
3. Near the cross! O Lamb of God, Bring its scenes be-fore me; Help me walk from
4. Near the cross I'll watch and wait, Hop-ing, trust-ing, ev - er, Till I reach the

CHORUS

heal - ing stream, Flows from Cal-v'ry's mountain.
Morn-ing Star Shed His beams a-round me.
day to day, With its shad-ows o'er me.
gold - en strand, Just be-yond the riv - er.

In the cross, in the cross,

Be my glo-ry ev - er, Till my raptured soul shall find Rest be-yond the riv - er.

225 A Beautiful Life

Wm. M. G.   Wm. M. Golden

1. Each day I'll do a gold-en deed, By help-ing those who are in need; My life on earth is but a span, And so I'll do the best I can, (the best I can).

2. To be a child of God each day, My light must shine a-long the way; I'll sing His praise while a-ges roll, And strive to help some trou-bled soul, (some trou-bled soul).

3. The on-ly life that will en-dure, Is one that's kind and good and pure; And so for God I'll take my stand, Each day I'll lend a help-ing hand, (a help-ing hand).

4. I'll help some-one in time of need, And jour-ney on with rap-id speed; I'll help the sick the poor and weak, And words of kind - ness to them speak, (kind words I'll speak).

5. While go-ing down life's wea-ry road, I'll try to lift some trav'ler's load; I'll try to turn the night to day, Make flow-ers bloom a-long the way, (the lone-ly way).

Refrain

Life's evening sun is sink-ing low, A few more days and I must go To meet the deeds that I have

Farther Along 226

Rev. W. B. Stevens
Arr. by J. R. Baxter, Jr.

W. B. S.

1. Tempt-ed and tried we're oft made to wonder Why it should be thus all the day
2. When death has come and taken our loved ones, It leaves our home so lone-ly and
3. Faith-ful till death said our lov-ing Mas-ter, A few more days to la-bor and
4. When we see Je-sus com-ing in glo-ry, When He comes from His home in the

long, While there are oth-ers liv-ing a-bout us, Nev-er mo-lest-ed
drear; Then do we won-der why oth-ers pros-per, Liv-ing so wick-ed
wait; Toils of the road will then seem as noth-ing, As we sweep thru the
sky; Then we shall meet Him in that bright mansion, We'll un-der-stand it

FINE   CHORUS   D. S.- We'll un-der-stand it

tho in the wrong.
year af-ter year.   Far-ther a-long we'll know all a-bout it, Far-ther a-
beau-ti-ful gate.
all by and by.

all by and by.   D. S.

long we'll un-der-stand why; Cheer up, my broth-er, live in the sun-shine,

227 I Belong To The King Of The Ages

S. R. A.

Stephen R. Adams

1. Down the hall-ways of ____ time there_ has ech-oed God's_
2. I was rest-less in my search to find a cor-ner of my

call To the lone-ly, ___ the lost ___ and op-pressed; - "You who___ are
own, And I need-ed just one chance to be-long; ___ Then He ___ took me

wea-ry, ___ just come un-to Me, ___ For I love you and I will
in ___ and He gave me a home, that's why I'm sing-ing this new and

CHORUS

give you rest." ___ I be - long to the King of the a - ges, ___ All the
glo-rious song! ___

trea-sures of His fam-'ly I share; ___ And when time has run its course

And they've closed the book of his-t'ry, I will still be a child in His care!__

A Song Within My Heart 228

W. E. M.

W. Elmo Mercer

1. There's a song with-in my heart, Such a love-ly mel-o-dy!
2. Now the sun-light of His love Shines up-on my up-ward way;
3. Most of all my voice I raise Thank-ing Him for sav-ing grace,

How it thrilled me from the start, It's a song of vic-to-ry.
Him a-lone I'm sing-ing of; He has turned my night to day.
I will ev-er sing His praise, And some day I'll see His face.

CHORUS

A song I'm sing - ing, Oh, may it nev-er de-part;
Yes, this song I glad-ly sing,

For Je - sus gives me This song with-in my heart.
For He a-lone has giv-en me

229 City Of Gold

S. C.

Shirley Cohron

1. There's a cit-y that looks o'er the val-ley of death, And its
2. There will be no more sor-row, pain, sick-ness or death, And the

glo-ry has nev-er been told;___ Where the Lamb is the light___
saints, they will nev-er grow old;___ How I long for that cit-y

in the midst of the night In that beau-ti-ful cit-y of gold.___
where there nev-er comes a night In that beau-ti-ful cit-y of gold.___

CHORUS

Where the sun___ nev-er sets,___ And the leaves___ nev-er

fade;_____ And the right-eous for-ev-er will shine like the

stars, In that beau - ti - ful cit - y of__ gold.___

How Firm A Foundation

Geo. Keith

1. How firm a foun-da-tion, ye saints of the Lord, Is laid for your
2. In ev - 'ry con-di - tion, in sick-ness, in health; In pov - er - ty's
3. "Fear not, I am with Thee, O be not dis-mayed, For I am thy
4. "The soul that on Je - sus still leans for re - pose, I will not, I

faith in His ex - cel - lent word! What more can He say than to
vale, or a-bound'-ing in wealth; At home and a - broad, on the
God, and will still give thee aid; I'll strength-en thee, help thee, and
will not, de - sert to His foes; That soul, though all hell should en-

you He hath said, You who un - to Je - sus for ref - uge have fled?
land, on the sea, "As thy days may de-mand, shall thy strength ev-er be."
cause thee to stand, Up - held by My right-eous, om-nip-o - tent hand.
deav - or to shake, I'll nev - er, no nev - er, no nev - er for - sake.

231 I Should Have Been Crucified

G. J.

Gordon Jensen

1. I was guilty with noth-ing to say, And they were com-ing to take me a - way, But then a voice from heaven was heard that said, "Let him go! Take me in-stead!"

2. Crown of thorns, the spear deep in His side, And the pain should have been mine, The rust-y nails were meant for me, (O,) yet Christ took them and let me go free!

CHORUS

And I should have been cru-ci-fied! I should have suf-fered and died! Oo I should have hung on the

cross in dis - grace, But Je - sus, God's Son, took my place!

Nothing But The Blood

232

R. L.

Robert Lowry

1. What can wash a - way my sins? Noth-ing but the blood of Je - sus;
2. For my par-don this I see, Noth-ing but the blood of Je - sus;
3. Noth-ing can for sin a - tone, Noth-ing but the blood of Je - sus;
4. This is all my hope and peace, Noth-ing but the blood of Je - sus;

What can make me whole a - gain? Noth-ing but the blood of Je - sus.
For my cleans-ing, this my plea, Noth-ing but the blood of Je - sus.
Naught of good that I have done, Noth-ing but the blood of Je - sus.
This is all my right-eous-ness, Noth-ing but the blood of Je - sus.

Chorus

Oh! pre - cious is the flow That makes me white as snow;

No oth - er fount I know, Noth-ing but the blood of Je - sus.

233 He Will Pilot Me

Charles T. Bailey

Byron L. Whitworth

1. Al-tho' I can-not see the way, O'er life's tem-pes-tuous
2. Dark clouds may gath-er in the sky, And rough the sea may
3. Dear Lord, what-e'er the storm may be, I'll sim-ply trust in

sea, dark sea, I know that Je-sus is my Friend, And that He'll
be, may be; His love shall ev-er be my song I know He'll
Thee, in Thee, Re-ly-ing on Thy love so true, To safe-ly

CHORUS

pi-lot me. By His hand He'll pi-lot me,
pi-lot me. He'll pi - lot me from

O-ver life's tem-pestuous sea, When my blind-ed eyes can't see,
day to day, When blind ed eyes can't

Can-not see the way, the way; Come what may, let
see the way; Let come what

come what may, On life's dark and storm-y sea, My dear Lord,
may on life's dark sea, My bless -

bless - ed Lord, He will pi-lot, pi-lot me.
ed Lord will pi - lot me.

234

Let The Lower Lights Be Burning

P. P. Bliss

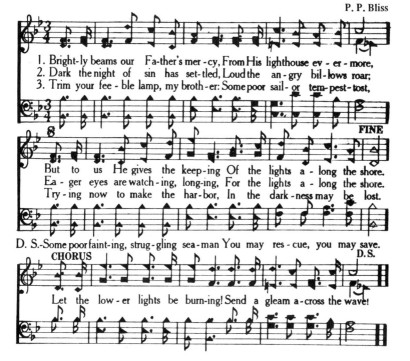

1. Bright-ly beams our Fa-ther's mer-cy, From His lighthouse ev - er - more,
2. Dark the night of sin has set-tled, Loud the an-gry bil-lows roar;
3. Trim your fee - ble lamp, my broth-er: Some poor sail- or tem-pest-tost,

FINE

But to us He gives the keep-ing Of the lights a - long the shore.
Ea - ger eyes are watch-ing, long-ing, For the lights a - long the shore.
Try - ing now to make the har-bor, In the dark-ness may be lost.

D. S.-Some poor faint-ing, strug-gling sea-man You may res - cue, you may save.

D.S.

CHORUS

Let the low - er lights be burn-ing! Send a gleam a-cross the wave!

235 I Just Came To Talk With You, Lord

D. R.

Dottie Rambo

1. I __ did-n't come here to ask You for an-y-thing. I just came to
2. (*Instruments play behind recitation to**)

talk with You, Lord__ You've an-swered a mil-lion pray'rs or more that

I for-got to thank You for, I just came to talk with You, Lord. _____

CHORUS

May-be to-mor-row there'll be trou-ble and sor-row, And a thou - sand

tear- drops may fall_____ But un-til I face to-mor - row's tasks, I have

no spec-ial fav-or to ask; I just came to talk with You, Lord.____

*RECITATION (2nd verse)

How many times, Lord, have troubles brought me down to my knees;
Oh, but this time I just came to talk with you, Lord;
You see, I have really no selfish motive in mind,
I just want to thank You, Lord, for all of the other times,
Oh, (to**)

Glory To His Name

236

Rev. E. A. Hoffman

Rev. J. H. Stockton

1. Down at the cross where my Sav-ior died, Down where for cleansing from
2. I am so won-drous-ly saved from sin, Je-sus so sweet-ly a-
3. Oh, precious foun-tain that saves from sin, I am so glad I have
4. Come to this foun-tain so rich and sweet; Cast thy poor soul at the

sin I cried, There to my heart was the blood ap-plied; Glo-ry to His name.
bides with-in, There at the cross where He took me in; Glo-ry to His name.
en-tered in; There Je-sus saves me and keeps me clean; Glo-ry to His name.
Sav-ior's feet; Plunge in to-day and be made com-plete; Glo-ry to His name.

Fine

D. S. There to my heart was the blood ap-plied; Glo-ry to His name.

Glo-ry to His name, Glo-ry to His name;

237 It's Different Now

Arr. by David Beatty

1. Once I was lost in sin, I had no peace with-in, To save my
2. I went to church one day to hear them sing and pray, The preach-er
3. Sin's fet-ters held me fast, the dye was al-most cast, My proud and
4. And now my hopes are bright, I praise Him day and night, How He could

wea-ry soul I knew not how; But Je-sus came to me, and
firm-ly plowed the gos-pel plow; He said you must re-pent, so
haugh-ty spir-it would not bow; But just one glimpse of Him, it
change me so I know not how; But praise the Lord it's done, the

by His grace I'm free,
down the aisle I went, Now it's dif-f'rent O so dif-f'rent
broke the pow'r of sin, yes, it's
vic-t'ry now is won,

CHORUS

now. It's dif-f'rent now, Since Je-sus saved my
Yes, it's dif-f'rent now,

soul, It's dif-f'rent now, since by His blood I'm
since He saved my soul, Yes, it's dif-f'rent now,

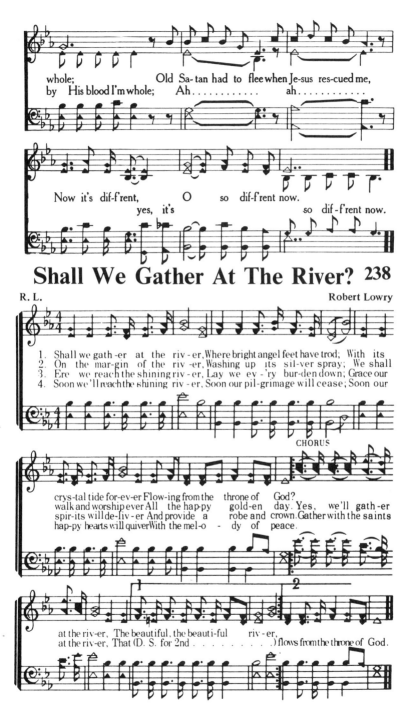

whole; Old Sa- tan had to flee when Je-sus res-cued me,
by His blood I'm whole; Ah............ ah............

Now it's dif-f'rent, O so dif-f'rent now.
yes, it's so dif-f'rent now.

Shall We Gather At The River? 238

R. L.   Robert Lowry

1. Shall we gath-er at the riv-er, Where bright angel feet have trod; With its
2. On the mar-gin of the riv-er, Washing up its sil-ver spray; We shall
3. Ere we reach the shining riv-er, Lay we ev-'ry bur-den down; Grace our
4. Soon we'll reach the shining riv-er, Soon our pil-grimage will cease; Soon our

CHORUS

crys-tal tide for-ev-er Flow-ing from the throne of God?
walk and worship ever All the hap-py gold-en day. Yes, we'll gath-er
spir-its will de-liv-er And provide a robe and crown. Gather with the saints
hap-py hearts will quiver With the mel-o - dy of peace.

1   2

at the riv-er, The beautiful, the beauti-ful riv-er,
at the riv-er, That (D. S. for 2nd . . . .) flows from the throne of God.

239
A Rich Man Am I

L. L.

Lowell Lundstrom

1. I found _____ some-thing that mon - ey can't buy, I found a gold
   I found a love _____ that's too sweet to tell, I found a faith
2. I found a dream _____ that's sure to come true, I found a rain-
   I found a song _____ the an - gels can sing, I found a way

mine be - yond the blue sky; I found a land where I'll live
_____ that's no wish - ing well; I found a life that I'll live
bow that's nev - er turned blue; I found a land where the tear-
to be rich as a king; I found a love that will burn

CHORUS

when I die,
till I die, I found the Lord, a rich man am I! Peo - ple
drops are dried,
till I die,

may say that I'm dream-ing a bit, But I like what I'm be-

liev - ing and I'm not gon - na quit! Yes, the Book told me that

I'll live when I die; I found the Lord, a rich man am I!

Saved Through Jesus' Blood 240

J. W. VanDeVenter
Arr. by John T. Benson, Jr.

J. W. D.

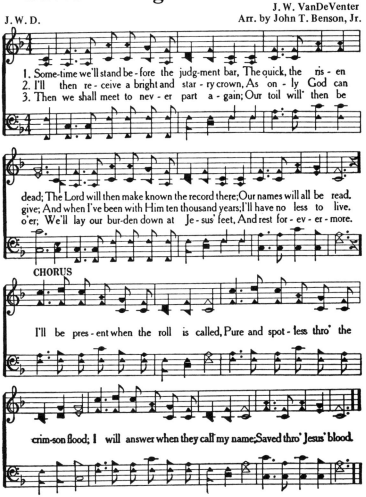

1. Some-time we'll stand be-fore the judg-ment bar, The quick, the ris - en
2. I'll then re - ceive a bright and star - ry crown, As on - ly God can
3. Then we shall meet to nev - er part a - gain; Our toil will then be

dead; The Lord will then make known the record there; Our names will all be read.
give; And when I've been with Him ten thousand years; I'll have no less to live.
o'er; We'll lay our bur-den down at Je - sus' feet, And rest for - ev - er-more.

CHORUS

I'll be pres - ent when the roll is called, Pure and spot - less thro' the

crim-son flood; I will answer when they call my name; Saved thro' Jesus' blood.

241 Something Worth Living For

Dale Oldham

William J. Gaither

1. Life was shat-tered and hope was gone Crush-ing the load that I bore,— Then out of the depths I cried, "O God, give me some-thing worth liv - ing for."—

2. There with life at its low - est ebb Who could heal and re - store?. Then He came and mend-ed my brok - en heart, He gave me some-thing worth liv - ing for.—

3. O the joy of sins for - giv'n, There's noth-ing the same as be - fore,— My life o - ver - flows since Je - sus came and gave me some-thing worth liv - ing for.—

CHORUS

Some - thing more than my yes - ter-days, More than I had be - fore Some - thing more than wealth or

Some-thing more than my yes-ter-days, More than I had, I had be - fore, Some-thing more wealth or

fame,
fame, He gave me some-thing worth liv - ing for.

All Hail The Power Of Jesus' Name

Edward Perrenet

Oliver Holden

1. All hail the pow'r of Je - sus' name! Let an - gels pros-trate fall!
2. Ye cho - sen seed of Is - rael's race, Ye ran-somed from the fall,
3. Let ev - 'ry kin - dred, ev - 'ry tribe, On this ter - res - trial ball,
4. O that with yon - der sa - cred throng, We at His feet may fall!

Bring forth the roy - al di - a - dem,
Hail Him who saves you by His grace, And crown Him Lord of all!
To Him all maj - es - ty as - cribe,
We'll join the ev - er - last - ing song,

Bring forth the roy - al di - a - dem,
Hail Him who saves you by His grace, And crown Him Lord of all!
To Him all maj - es - ty as - cribe,
We'll join the ev - er - last - ing song,

243 One More Time

W. E. M.

W. Elmo Mercer

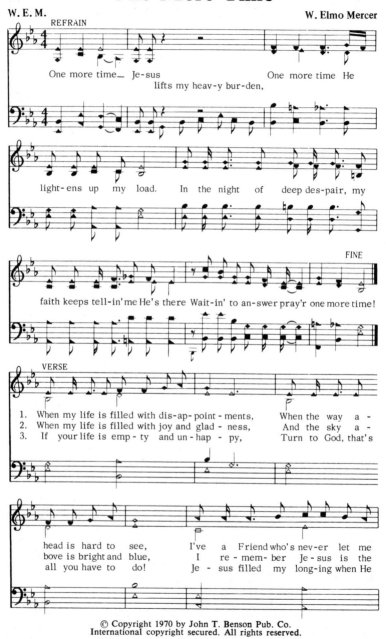

REFRAIN

One more time— Je-sus
lifts my heav-y bur-den,
One more time He

light-ens up my load. In the night of deep des-pair, my

faith keeps tell-in' me He's there Wait-in' to an-swer pray'r one more time!

VERSE

1. When my life is filled with dis-ap-point-ments,
2. When my life is filled with joy and glad-ness,
3. If your life is emp-ty and un-hap-py,

When the way a-
And the sky a-
Turn to God, that's

head is hard to see,
bove is bright and blue,
all you have to do!

I've a Friend who's nev-er let me
I re-mem-ber Je-sus is the
Je-sus filled my long-ing when He

down yet,   I just pray and ask Him to   help me. _____
rea - son,   For He helped me when I asked Him to. _____
saved me,   And I know He'll do the same for you. _____

D.C.

Shake Hands With Mother Again 244

W. A. B.   W. A. Berry

1. If   I should be liv - ing when Je - sus comes And could know the day
2. I'd like to say "Moth - er, this is your boy, You   left when you
3. There's com - ing a time when I can go home To   meet my
4. There'll be no more sor - row or pain to bear In   that home be-

and   the hour, I'd like to be stand - ing at moth - er's   tomb
went   a - way; And now my dear moth - er it gives me great joy
loved ones up there; There I can see Je - sus up - on His   throne
yond   the sky; O glo - ri - ous tho't when we all get   there,

FINE   CHORUS

When Je - sus comes in His pow'r.
To   see you a - gain to - day."   'Twill be a won - der - ful hap - py day
In   that bright cit - y, so fair.
We   nev - er will say "good - by."

D. S. - "Shake hands with mother a - gain."   D. S.

Up there on the gold - en strand; When I can hear Je - sus my Sav - ior   say,

245

Sunrise

G. J.

Gordon Jensen

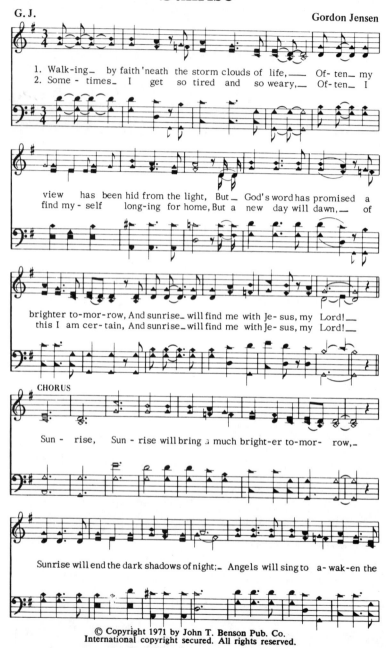

1. Walk-ing by faith 'neath the storm clouds of life, Of-ten my
2. Some-times I get so tired and so weary, Of-ten I

view has been hid from the light, But God's word has promised a
find my-self long-ing for home, But a new day will dawn, of

brighter to-mor-row, And sunrise will find me with Je-sus, my Lord!
this I am cer-tain, And sunrise will find me with Je-sus, my Lord!

CHORUS

Sun - rise, Sun - rise will bring a much bright-er to-mor- row,

Sunrise will end the dark shadows of night; Angels will sing to a-wak-en the

dawn-ing, Sun - rise, Sun - rise will find me with Je-sus, my Lord!

Where The Spirit Of The Lord Is 246

S. R. A.

Stephen R. Adams

Where the Spirit of the Lord is, there is peace!___ Where the
there is peace!

Spir-it of the Lord is, there is love!___ There is comfort in life's
there is love!

dark-est ho-ur, there is light and life, There is help and power in the

Spir - it, in the Spir - it of the Lord!___
of the Lord!

247 Just Over In The Gloryland

Jas. W. Acuff

Emmett S. Dean

1. I've a home pre-pared where the saints a-bide, Just o - ver in the
2. I am on my way to those mansions fair, Just o - ver in the
3. What a joy - ful tho't, that my Lord I'll see, Just o - ver in the
4. With the blood-washed throng I will shout and sing, Just o - ver in the

glo - ry-land; And I long to be by my Sav-ior's side, Just
glo - ry-land; There to sing God's praise, and His glo - ry share, Just
glo - ry-land; And with kin-dred saved, there for - ev - er be, Just
glo - ry-land; Glad ho - san - nas to Christ, the Lord and King, Just

REFRAIN.

o - ver in the glo - ry - land. Just o - ver in the glo - ry-land,
Just o - ver, o - ver in the glo - ry-land,

I'll join........ the hap - py an - gel band, Just o - ver in the
I'll join, yes, join the hap - py an - gel band,

glo - ry - land; Just o - ver in the glo - ry - land, There
Just o - ver, o - ver in the glo - ry - land, There

with........ the might-y host I'll stand, Just o - ver in the glo - ry land.
yes, with

My Home, Sweet Home 248

N. B. V.

N. B. Vandall

1. Walk-ing a-long life's road one day, I heard a voice so sweet-ly say, "A
2. Loved ones up-on that shore I'll meet, Casting their crowns at Je-sus' feet; I'll
3. Life's day is short, I soon must go, To be with Him Who loved me so; I

place up in heav'n I am building thee, A beau-ti-ful, beau-ti-ful home."
worship and praise Him for ever-more, In my beau-ti-ful, beau-ti-ful home.
see in the distance that shining shore, My beau-ti-ful, beau-ti-ful home.

CHORUS

Home, sweet home, home, sweet home, Where I'll nev - er roam;

I see the light of that cit - y so bright, My home, sweet home.

249 Someday

C. W. and P. D.

Clarence Williams & Paul Davis

1. __ Sometimes there are bur-dens too heavy to bear, But__ there'll
2. Well, I may not have much down here to show, But I'll walk on

be no more someday;___ __ Sometimes in this old life, there are
streets of gold someday;___ In my Fa-ther's__ house, there are

heartaches, there are tears; But they'll all be wiped a- way__ someday!
rich- es un - told; And__ I'll__ share it all__ someday!__

CHORUS

Some- day, ___ Some- day, ___ { I'll__
In the morn-ing, No more tears__ { Oh, I'll

leave it all be-hind some- day;__ } Some- day, ___
walk on streets of gold some- day;__ } No more heart- aches__

Some- day.____ { All Heav-en will be mine_ some day.___
No more sor-row, { Oh won - der ful home_ some day.__

I Would Not Be Denied   250

C. P. Jones

1. When pangs of death seized on my soul, Un - to the Lord I cried,
2. As Ja - cob in the days of old, I wres-tled with the Lord;
3. Old Sa - tan said my Lord was gone, And would not hear my prayer;

Till Je - sus came and made me whole; I would not be de - nied.
And in - stant, with a cour-age bold, I stood up - on His word.
But, praise the Lord! the work is done, And Christ the Lord is here.

CHORUS.

I would not be de - nied (de-nied), I would not be de - nied (de-nied),

Till Je - sus came and made me whole; I would not be de - nied.
de-nied.

251 To Be Like Jesus

2nd verse by Gloria Gaither

Henry Slaughter
Arr. by Henry Slaughter

1. He lift-ed up the fall-en man,__ He gave the world a
2. His look of love went ev-'ry-where,__ And lives were changed when

helping hand, His heart was touched each time He saw a soul in need.__
He was there, Hun-gry eyes and hun-gry souls felt His em-brace.__

Dis-played __ kind-ness ev - 'ry- where, Mer-cy and love was His to
He stooped to mend each crip-pled child,_ His heal-ing touch was strong but

CHORUS

share, and like this Man of Gal-i-lee I want to be. ___ To be like Je-sus,_
mild, and like this Man of Gal-i-lee I want to be. ___

___ To be like Je-sus,__ All I ask __ to be like Him._All thro' life's

jour-ney___ from earth to Glo-ry,___ All I ask,___ To be like Him.___

Look And Live

W. A. O.

W. A. Ogden

1. I've a message from the Lord, Hal-le-lu-jah! The message un-to you I'll give;
2. I've a message full of love, Hal-le-lu-jah! A message, O my friend, for you;
3. Life is of-fered un-to you, Hal-le-lu-jah! E - ter-nal life thy soul shall have,
4. I will tell you how I came, Hal-le-lu-jah! To Jesus when He made me whole:

'T is re-cord-ed in His word, Hal-le - lu - jah! It is on-ly that you "look and live."
'T is a message from above, Hal-le - lu - jah! Je-sus said it, and I know 'tis true.
If you'll on-ly look to Him, Hal-le - lu - jah! Look to Jesus, who a-lone can save.
'T was believing on His name, Hal-le - lu - jah! I trusted, and He saved my soul.

D.S.—'T is recorded in His word, Hal-le - lu - jah! It is on - ly that you "look and live."

CHORUS.

"Look and live,"......my brother, live,   Look to Je-sus now and live;
"Look and live," my brother, live, "Look and live,"

253 Ten Thousand Angels

R. O.

Ray Overholt

1. They bound the hands of Je-sus in the gar-den where He prayed; They
2. Up - - on His pre-cious head they placed a crown of thorns; They
3. When they nailed Him to the Cross, His moth-er stood near-by; He
4. To the howl-ing mob He yield-ed; He did not for mer-cy cry. The

led Him thro the streets in shame. They said, "Cru-ci-fy Him; He's to blame.
laughed and said, "Be-hold the King." They struck Him and they cursed Him and
said, "Wom-an, be-hold thy son!" He cried, "I thirst for wa-ter," but they
Cross of shame He took a-lone. And when He cried, "It's fin-ished," He

pure and free from sin; They said, "Cru-ci-fy Him; He's to blame.
mocked His ho-ly name. All a-lone He suf-fered ev-'ry-thing.
gave Him none to drink. Then the sin-ful work of man was done.
gave him-self to die; Sal - - va-tion's won-drous plan was done.

CHORUS
f Faster

He could have called ten thou-sand an-gels To de-stroy the

world and set Him free. He could have called,
the world

ten thou - sand an - gels, But He died a - lone, for you and me.
a - lone

Jesus Sets My Heart To Singing 254

W. E. M.
W. Elmo Mercer

1. Deep with in my heart a mel - o - dy keeps com-ing back to me;
2. Though sometimes my life be dark and drear - y and the way so long;
3. Drink - ing at the fount of liv - ing wa - ter I found peace and love;

It's a song of gladness, Nev - er one of sad-ness, And it gives me vic-
Je - sus stands be- side me, He will ev - er guide me, Through the night He gives
All the world for- sak- ing, Je - sus hum-bly tak- ing, Now my home is heav'n

CHORUS

to - ry.
a song. Je - sus sets my heart to sing-ing, Singing ev-'ry-where I go;
a- bove.

He can start the joy bells ring-ing When He whis-pers sweet and low.
sweet and low.

255 I'll Live In Glory

J. M. H.

J. M. Henson

1. I'd like to stay here long-er than man's al-lot-ted days, And watch the fleeting
2. I want to be of serv-ice a-long this pilgrim way, And lead the lost to
3. The end I know is near-ing, by faith I look a-way, To yon-der home su-

chang-es of life's un-e-ven ways; But if my Sav-ior calls me to
Je - sus as fer-vent-ly I pray; As day by day I trav-el I'll
per - nal, the land of end-less day; I'll cling to Him for-ev-er and

that sweet home on high, I'll live with Him for-ev-er in glo-ry by and by.
keep Him ev-er nigh, And live with Him for-ev-er in glo-ry by and by.
look be-yond the sky, And live with Him for-ev-er in glo-ry by and by.

CHORUS

O yes, I'll live in glo-ry by and by, I'll tell and sing love's
live in glo-ry by and by,

sto - ry there on high; There with my dear Redeem-er no
tell love's sto-ry there on high; there no

more to die, O yes, I'll live in glo-ry by and by.
no more to die, glo-ry by and by.

Ship Ahoy

256

M. J. Cartwright

D. B. Towner

'Effective Solo

1. I was drift-ing a-way on' life's pit-i-less sea, And the
2. 'Twas the "Old ship of Zi-on," thus sail-ing a-long, All a-
3. The good Cap-tain com-mand-ed a boat to be low'red, And with
4. O soul, sink-ing down 'neath sin's mer-ci-less wave, The strong

an-gry waves threatened my ru-in to be, When a-way at my side, there I
board her seemed joyous, I heard their sweet song; And the Captain's kind ear, ev-er
ten-der com-pas-sion He took me on board; And I'm hap-py to-day, all my
arm of our Cap-tain is might-y to save; Then trust Him to-day, no

dim-ly des-cried A state-ly old ves-sel, and loud-ly I cried:
read-y to hear, Caught my wail of dis-tress, as I cried out in fear:
sins washed a-way In the blood of my Sav-ior, and now I can say:
long-er de-lay, Board the old ship of Zi-on, and shout on your way:

"Ship a-hoy! Ship a-hoy!" And loud-ly I cried: "Ship a-hoy!"
"Ship a-hoy! Ship a-hoy!" As I cried out in fear: "Ship a-hoy!"
"Bless the Lord! Bless the Lord!" From my soul I can say: Bless the Lord!"
"Je-sus saves! Je-sus saves!" Shout and sing on your way: "Jesus saves!"

257 God Said It, I Believe It, That Settles It

Stephen Adams
& Gene Braun

Stephen Adams

1. "Faith is the es-sence of things un- seen,__ The sub-stance of things
2. God is the au-thor and He's the ending of _ all that I be -

hoped for." God's Word has said it, and I be - lieve it, For the
lieve in. Life more a - bun-dant is yours for the ask-ing: _ The

CHORUS

mir-a-cle has hap-pened to me! God said it, and I be-lieve it, and that
mir-a-cle can hap-pen to you!

set-tles it for me! God said it, and I be-lieve it,— and that set-tles it for

me! Though some may doubt that His Word is_ true, I've chosen to be-lieve it,

Now, how a-bout you? God said it, and I be-lieve it, and that settles it for me!

Sweet Hour Of Prayer 258

W. W. Walford

Wm. B. Bradbury

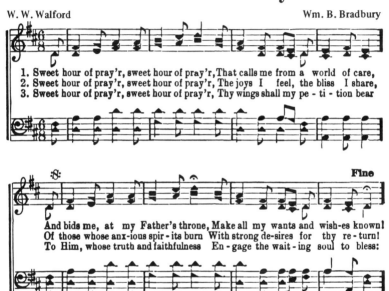

1. Sweet hour of pray'r, sweet hour of pray'r, That calls me from a world of care,
2. Sweet hour of pray'r, sweet hour of pray'r, The joys I feel, the bliss I share,
3. Sweet hour of pray'r, sweet hour of pray'r, Thy wings shall my pe - ti - tion bear

And bids me, at my Father's throne, Make all my wants and wish-es known!
Of those whose anx-ious spir-its burn With strong de-sires for thy re-turn!
To Him, whose truth and faithfulness En - gage the wait - ing soul to bless:

D. S.—And oft es-capes the tempter's snare By the re-turn, sweet hour of pray'r.
D. S.—And glad-ly take my sta - tion there, And wait for thee, sweet hour of pray'r.
D. S.—I'll cast on Him my ev - 'ry care, And wait for thee, sweet hour of pray'r.

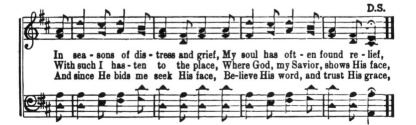

In sea - sons of dis - tress and grief, My soul has oft - en found re - lief,
With such I has - ten to the place, Where God, my Savior, shows His face,
And since He bids me seek His face, Be-lieve His word, and trust His grace,

259 The Fire Song

Unknown

Arr. by Mrs. James A. Pate

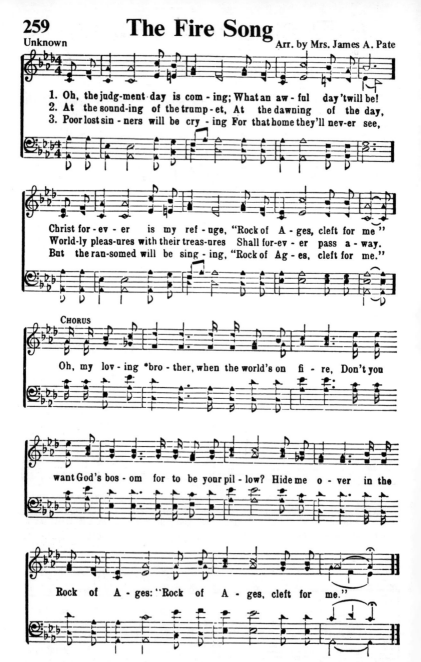

1. Oh, the judg-ment day is com - ing; What an aw - ful day 'twill be!
2. At the sound-ing of the trump - et, At the dawning of the day,
3. Poor lost sin - ners will be cry - ing For that home they'll nev - er see,

Christ for - ev - er is my ref - uge, "Rock of A - ges, cleft for me"
World-ly pleas-ures with their treas-ures Shall for-ev - er pass a - way.
But the ran-somed will be sing - ing, "Rock of Ag - es, cleft for me."

CHORUS

Oh, my lov - ing *bro - ther, when the world's on fi - re, Don't you

want God's bos - om for to be your pil - low? Hide me o - ver in the

Rock of A - ges: "Rock of A - ges, cleft for me."

Just A Closer Walk With Thee 260

Anonymous

Arr. W. E. Mercer

1. I am weak but Thou art strong (Thou art strong), Je - sus keep me from all
2. Thru this world of toil and snares (toil and snares), If I fal - ter, Lord, who
3. When my fee - ble life is o'er (life is o'er), Time for me will be no

wrong (from all wrong); I'll be sat - is-fied as long (just as long), As I walk let me
cares (Lord, who cares)? Who with me my burden shares (burden shares)? None but Thee, dear
more (be no more); Guide me gently, safely o'er (safely o'er), To Thy king-dom

CHORUS.

walk close to Thee (close to Thee).
Lord, none but Thee (none but Thee). Just a closer walk with Thee (walk with Thee),
shore, to Thy shore (to Thy shore).

Grant it, Je - sus, is my plea (hum - ble plea); Dai - ly walk-ing close to

Thee (close to Thee), Let it be, dear Lord, let it be (let it be).

261 Ever Gentle, Ever Sweet

Stephen R. Adams

© Copyright 1971 by Dimension Music Company.
International copyright secured. All rights reserved.

When The Saints Go Marching In

262

Verses by
John T. Benson, Jr.

Chorus Traditional

Arr. by H. F. Hammond

1. I'm a pil-grim and a stran-ger Wan-d'ring thro' this world of sin,
2. Oh, I know I'll see my Sav-iour If my life is free from sin,
3. When we gath-er 'round the Throne And the gates are closed with-in,
4. I'm wait-ing for the char-iot To swing low and I'll step in.

On my way to that fair cit-y, When the Saints go marching in.
Heav-en's doors will o-pen for me When the Saints go marching in.
I'll be shout-ing "Glo-ry, Glo-ry" When the Saints go marching in.
On the clouds I'll ride to Heav-en When the Saints go marching in;

CHORUS

When the saints go marching in, When the saints go
(When the saints marching in, Saints go)

march-ing in; Lord I want to be in that
(march-ing in go march-ing in O)

num-ber When the saints go march-ing in.
(that num-ber, Saints go march-ing in go march-ing in.)

count-less num-ber.

263 I Feel Like Shoutin'

W. E. M.

W. Elmo Mercer

CHORUS

D.C. I feel like shoutin'___ like shoutin' glo -ry to the Lord, Glory to the

Lord for -ev -er-more_____ Feel like sing -in'___ Like singin' prais -es

FINE Verse

to His name; Praises like I nev-er sung before _____ 1. Sun-day's a fine day
2. Some morning yonder

just to praise the Lord, Gather in the church and listen to His word__And
heaven's gates of pearl Will swing open for me as I leave this world__Then

D.C.

then on Monday, tho' the skies be gray, He'll send the sunshine that will make you say;
while the a -ges roll I'll be at home With friends and loved ones all around God's throne.

The Great Speckled Bird

264

Traditional

Arr. by W. Elmo Mercer

1. What a beau-ti-ful thought I am think-ing____ Con-cern-ing the great Speck-led Bird; ____ Re-mem-ber her name is re-cord-ed ____ On the pag-es of God's Ho-ly Word. ____ De-sir-ing to low-er her stand-ard, ____ They watch ev'ry move that she makes; __ For they long to find fault with her teaching, ____ But real-ly they find _ no mis-take. ____

2. In the presence of all her de-spis-ers, __ With a song nev-er ut-tered be-fore; ____ She will rise and be gone in a moment, ____ 'Til the great trib-u-la-tions are o'er. ____ I am glad I have learned of her meek-ness, __ I am proud that my name is on her book; __ For I want to be one nev-er fear-ing __ On the face of my Sav-ior to look. ____

3. Her ____ wings shelter men of all na-tions, . ____ Of earth's ev-'ry col-or and race; ____ She has gathered them all in her keep-ing ____ To pre-sent to the Lord face to face. ____ When Christ cometh descend-ing from heav-en, __ On the clouds as He writes in His Word; __ I'll be joy-ful-ly car-ried to meet Him _ On the wings of the great Speckled Bird. ____

265 Kneel At The Cross

Chas E. Moody

Chas E. Moody
Arr. Chas E Moody

1. Kneel at the cross, Christ will meet you there, Come while He waits for you;
2. Kneel at the cross, There is room for all Who would His glo - ry share;
3. Kneel at the cross, Give your i - dols up, Look un - to realms a - bove;

List to His voice, Leave with Him your care And be-gin life a-new
Bliss there a-waits, Harm can ne'er be-fall Those who are anchored there.
Turn not a-way To life's sparkling cup, Trust only in His love.

CHORUS

Kneel.......... at the cross,...... Leave.......
Kneel at the cross, Kneel at the cross, Leave ev-'ry care

ev-'ry care;........... .... Kneel........... at the
Leave ev-'ry care; Kneel at the cross,

cross .... Je-sus will meet you there... ....
Kneel at the cross, meet you there.

Gathering Flowers
For The Master's Bouquet

M. E. B.

Marvin E. Baumgardner

1. Death is an an-gel sent down from a-bove, Sent for the buds and the flow-ers we love; Tru-ly 'tis so, for in heav-en's own way Each soul is a flow'r in the Mas-ter's bouquet.
2. Loved ones are passing each day and each hour, Pass-ing a-way "as the life of a flow'r;" But ev-'ry bud and each blos-som some day Will bloom as a flow'r in the Mas-ter's bouquet.
3. Let us be faith-ful till life's work is done, Bloom-ing with love till the reap-er shall come; Then we'll be gath-ered to-geth-er for aye, Trans-plant-ed to bloom in the Mas-ter's bouquet.

Chorus

Gath-er-ing flow'rs for the Mas-ter's bouquet, Beau-ti-ful flow'rs that will nev-er de-cay; Gath-ered by an-gels and carried a-way For-ev-er to bloom in the Master's bouquet.

267 Then Why The Tears?

L.W.

Lanny Wolfe

1. Has He ev-er failed to see you through in your dark-est hour?
2. When it seemed your heart would almost break, did He com-fort you?

___ Has the Sav-ior ev-er failed to be your strong and ___
And when it seemed your load was more than you could take, did He

might-y tow'r? ___ Has He ev-er left you in
lift it for you? ___ When you thought you car-ried your

your des-pair? When you called on Him, ___ did you find Him there? Has He
cross a-lone, Did you hear Him say, "You're not on your own?" ___ Has He

ev-er failed you, child of God, Has He ev-er failed you yet? ___
ev- er failed you one ___ time, Has He ev-er failed you yet? ___

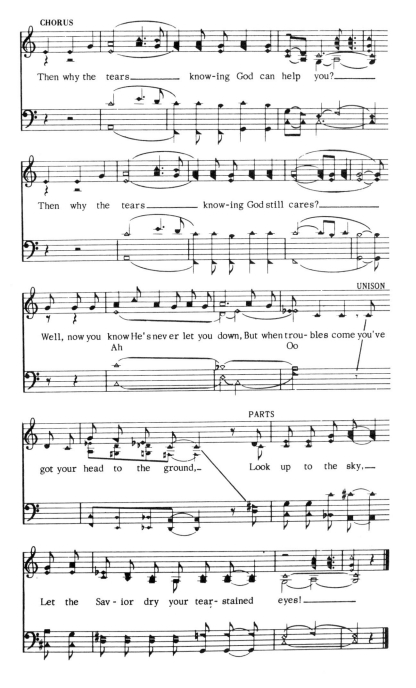

CHORUS

Then why the tears_____ know-ing God can help you?_____

Then why the tears_____ know-ing God still cares?_____

UNISON

Well, now you know He's nev er let you down, But when trou- bles come you've
Ah   Oo

PARTS

got your head to the ground,— Look up to the sky,—

Let the Sav - ior dry your tear- stained eyes!_____

268

William J.
& Gloria Gaither

Gentle Shepherd

William J. Gaither

Gen - tle Shep - herd, ___ come and lead us, ___ For we

need You to help us find our way. ___ Gen - tle

Shep - herd, ___ come and feed us, ___ For we need Your strength from

day to day; ___ There's no oth - er ___ we can turn to ___

Who can help us face an - oth - er day; ___ Gen - tle

Jesus, We Just Want To Thank You

269

William J.
& Gloria Gaither

William J. Gaither

1. Je-sus, we just want to thank You, __ Je-sus, we just want to
2. Je-sus, we just want to praise You, __ Je-sus, we just want to

thank __ You; Je-sus, we just want to thank You, __ Thank You for
praise __ You; Je-sus, we just want to praise You, __ Praise You for

1. **2.**

be-ing so good. __

3. Je - sus, we just want to
4. Sav - iour, we just want to
5. Je - sus, we know You are

tell You; __ Je - sus, we just want to tell __ You, Je - sus, we
serve You; __ Sav - iour, we just want to serve __ You, Sav - iour, we
com - ing, __ Je - sus, we know You are com - ing; Je - sus, we

just want to tell You, __ We love You for be - ing so good. __
just want to serve You, __ ⅞ __ Serve You for be - ing so good. __
know You are com - ing, __ ⅞ __ Take us to live in Your home. __

270 I'll Live On

T. J. L.

Thos. J. Laney

1. 'Tis a sweet and glo-rious tho't that comes to me, I'll live on,
2. When my bod-y's slum-b'ring in the cold, cold clay,
3. When the world's on fire, and dark-ness veils the sun,
4. In the glo-ry land with Je-sus on the throne, I'll live on

Yes, I'll live on; Je-sus saved my soul from death and now I'm free,
Yes, I'll live on; There to sleep in Je-sus till the judg-ment day,
Yes, I'll live on; Men will cry and to the rocks and moun-tains run,
Yes, I'll live on; For e-ter-nal a-ges sing-ing home, sweet home,

CHORUS

I'll live on, yes, I'll live on. I'll live on, yes, I'll live
I'll live on, on, on,

on, on, on, In e-ter-ni-ty I'll live on and on; I'll live on, on, on,

Yes, I'll live on and on, In e-ter-ni-ty I'll live on, yes, I'll live on.

271 Hallelujah, We Shall Rise

J. E. Thomas
Last verse by R. E. W.

J. E. Thomas

Not too fast

1. In the res-ur-rec-tion morn-ing, When the trump of God shall sound,
2. In the res-ur-rec-tion morn-ing, What a meet-ing it will be,
3. In the res-ur-rec-tion morn-ing, Bless-ed tho't it is to me,
4. In the res-ur-rec-tion morn-ing, We shall meet Him in the air,

We shall rise,   we shall rise! Then the saints will come re-joic-ing,
When our fa-thers and our moth-ers,
I shall see my bless-ed Sav-ior
Hal-le-lu-jah!   And be car-ried up to glo-ry

FINE

And no tears will e'er be found, We shall rise,   we shall rise!
And our loved ones we shall see,
Who so free-ly died for me,
To our home so bright and fair,   Hal-le-lu-jah!

D. S.-Hal-le-lujah! in that morning we shall rise.

CHORUS

Hal-le-lu-jah!   Amen! We shall rise!   Hal-le-lu-jah!
We shall rise,   we shall rise!

D. S.

In the res-ur-rec-tion morn-ing, When death's pris-on bars are brok-en,

Do, Lord

The Church In The Wildwood 273

W. S. P.

Dr. Wm. S. Pitts

1. There's a church in the val-ley by the wild-wood, No love-li-er
2. Oh, come to the church in the wild-wood, To the trees where the
3. How sweet on a clear Sab-bath morn-ing, To list to the
4. From the church in the val-ley by the wild-wood, When day fades a-

spot in the dale; No place is so dear to my child-hood As the
wild flow-ers bloom; Where the part-ing hymn will be chant-ed, We will
clear ring-ing bell; Its tones so sweet-ly are call-ing, Oh,
way in-to night, I would fain from this spot of my child-hood Wing my

D.S.—No spot is so dear to my child-hood As the

FINE   CHORUS

lit-tle brown church in the vale.
weep by the side of the tomb.
come to the church in the vale.   Come to the
way to the man-sions of light.   Oh, come, come, come, come, come, come,

lit-tle brown church in the vale.

D.S.

church in the wild - wood, Oh, come to the church in the vale;
come, come, come, come, come, come, come, come, come, come, come, come, come;

274
Jesus Is Lord Of All

William J.
& Gloria Gaither

William J. Gaither

1. All my to-mor - rows, all my past,
2. All of my con - flicts, all my thoughts, Je-sus is Lord ___
3. All of my long - ings, all my dreams,

of all. ___ 1. I've quit my strug - gles, content-ment at last,
2. His love wins the bat - tles I could not have fought,
3. All ___ my fail - ures His pow - er re - deems,

CHORUS:

Je - sus is Lord ___ of all. ___ King of kings, Lord of lords,

Je - sus is Lord ___ of all; ___ All my pos - sess - ions, and

all my life, Je - sus is Lord ___ of all. ___

Battle Hymn Of The Republic 275

Julia Ward Howe

William Steffe

1. Mine eyes have seen the glo-ry of the com-ing of the Lord; He is
2. I have seen Him in the watch-fires of a hundred circling camps; They have
3. He has sounded forth the trumpet that shall nev-er sound re-treat; He is
4. In the beau-ty of the lil-ies Christ was born a-cross the sea, With a

trampling out the vintage where the grapes of wrath are stored; He hath loosed the
build-ed Him an al-tar in the evening dews and damps; I can read His
sift-ing out the hearts of men be-fore His judgment seat. O be swift, my
glo-ry in His bos-om that trans-fig-ures you and me; As He died to

fate-ful lightning of His ter-ri-ble swift sword; His truth is marching on.
righteous sentence by the dim and flar-ing lamps; His day is marching on.
soul, to an-swer Him! be ju-bi-lant, my feet! Our God is marching on.
make men ho-ly, let us die to make men free; While God is marching on.

Glo-ry! glo-ry, hal-le-lu-jah! Glo-ry! glo-ry, hal-le-lu-jah! His truth is marching on.
Glo-ry! glo-ry, hal-le-lu-jah! Glo-ry! glo-ry, hal-le-lu-jah! His day is marching on.
Glo-ry! glo-ry, hal-le-lu-jah! Glo-ry! glo-ry, hal-le-lu-jah! Our God is marching on.
Glo-ry! glo-ry, hal-le-lu-jah! Glo-ry! glo-ry, hal-le-lu-jah! While God is march-ing on.

276 Joy To The World

Isaac Watts

George F. Handel

1. Joy to the world! the Lord is come; Let earth re-ceive her King; Let ev-ery heart pre-pare Him room, And heaven and na-ture sing, And heaven and na-ture sing, And heav-en, and heaven and na-ture sing.

2. Joy to the earth! the Sav-iour reigns; Let men their songs em-ploy; While fields and floods, rocks, hills and plains Re-peat the sound-ing joy, Re-peat the sound-ing joy, Re-peat, re-peat the sound-ing joy.

3. No more let sins and sor-rows grow, Nor thorns in-fest the ground; He comes to make His bless-ings flow Far as the curse is found, Far as the curse is found, Far as, far as the curse is found.

4. He rules the world with truth and grace, And makes the na-tions prove The glo-ries of His right-eous-ness, And won-ders of His love, And won-ders of His love, And won-ders, and won-ders of His love.

1. And heaven and na-ture sing, ... And heaven and na-ture sing,

O Little Town Of Bethlehem 277

278 Hark, The Herald Angels Sing

Charles Wesley

Felix Mendelssohn

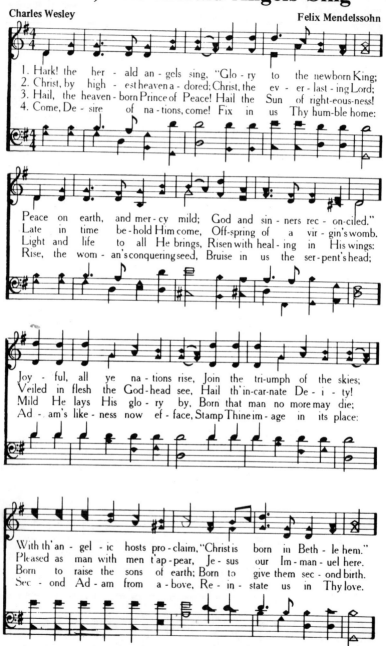

1. Hark! the her - ald an - gels sing, "Glo - ry to the newborn King;
2. Christ, by high - est heaven a - dored; Christ, the ev - er - last - ing Lord;
3. Hail, the heaven - born Prince of Peace! Hail the Sun of right-eous-ness!
4. Come, De - sire of na - tions, come! Fix in us Thy hum-ble home:

Peace on earth, and mer - cy mild; God and sin - ners rec - on-ciled."
Late in time be - hold Him come, Off-spring of a vir - gin's womb.
Light and life to all He brings, Risen with heal - ing in His wings:
Rise, the wom - an's conquering seed, Bruise in us the ser-pent's head;

Joy - ful, all ye na - tions rise, Join the tri-umph of the skies;
Veiled in flesh the God-head see, Hail th' in-car-nate De - i - ty!
Mild He lays His glo - ry by, Born that man no more may die;
Ad - am's like - ness now ef - face, Stamp Thine im - age in its place:

With th' an - gel - ic hosts pro - claim, "Christ is born in Beth - le hem."
Pleased as man with men t'ap - pear, Je - sus our Im - man - uel here.
Born to raise the sons of earth; Born to give them sec - ond birth.
Sec - ond Ad - am from a - bove, Re - in - state us in Thy love.

Hark! the her - ald an - gels sing, "Glo - ry to the newborn King."

Silent Night

279

Joseph Mohr

Franz Gruber

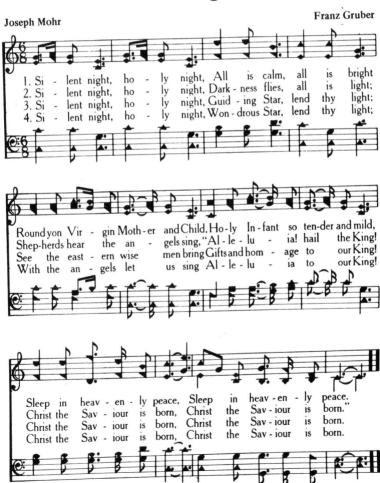

1. Si - lent night, ho - ly night, All is calm, all is bright
2. Si - lent night, ho - ly night, Dark - ness flies, all is light;
3. Si - lent night, ho - ly night, Guid - ing Star, lend thy light;
4. Si - lent night, ho - ly night, Won - drous Star, lend thy light;

Round yon Vir - gin Moth - er and Child, Ho - ly In - fant so ten-der and mild,
Shep-herds hear the an - gels sing, "Al - le - lu - ia! hail the King!
See the east - ern wise men bring Gifts and hom - age to our King!
With the an - gels let us sing Al - le - lu - ia to our King!

Sleep in heav - en - ly peace, Sleep in heav - en - ly peace.
Christ the Sav - iour is born, Christ the Sav - iour is born.
Christ the Sav - iour is born, Christ the Sav - iour is born.
Christ the Sav - iour is born, Christ the Sav - iour is born.

280 O Come, All Ye Faithful

Tr. by Frederick Oakeley

Wade's Cantus Diversi

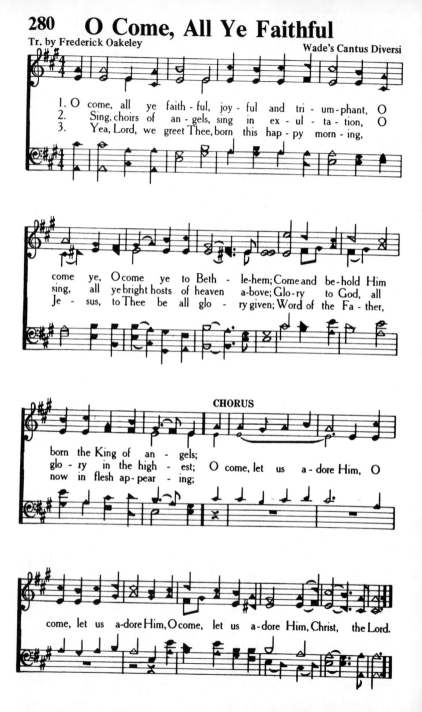

1. O come, all ye faith-ful, joy-ful and tri-um-phant, O
2. Sing, choirs of an-gels, sing in ex-ul-ta-tion, O
3. Yea, Lord, we greet Thee, born this hap-py morn-ing,

come ye, O come ye to Beth - le-hem; Come and be-hold Him
sing, all ye bright hosts of heaven a-bove; Glo-ry to God, all
Je - sus, to Thee be all glo - ry given; Word of the Fa - ther,

CHORUS

born the King of an - gels;
glo - ry in the high - est; O come, let us a-dore Him, O
now in flesh ap-pear - ing;

come, let us a-dore Him, O come, let us a-dore Him, Christ, the Lord.

RESPONSIVE READINGS

281   Adoration

Psalms 8

O Lord our Lord, how excellent is thy name in all the earth!

Who hast set thy glory above the heavens.

Out of the mouth of babes and sucklings hast thou ordained strength because of thine enemies, that thou mightest still the enemy and the avenger.

When I consider thy heavens, the work of thy fingers, the moon and the stars, which thou hast ordained;

What is man, that thou art mindful of him? and the son of man, that thou visitest him?

For thou hast made him a little lower than the angels, and hast crowned him with glory and honour.

Thou madest him to have dominion over the works of thy hands; thou hast put all things under his feet:

All sheep and oxen, yea, and the beasts of the field;

The fowl of the air, and the fish of the sea, and whatsoever passeth through the paths of the seas.

O Lord our Lord, how excellent is thy name in all the earth!

282   Praise

Psalms 96: 1-10

O sing unto the Lord a new song: sing unto the Lord, all the earth.

Sing unto the Lord, bless his name; shew forth his salvation from day to day.

Declare his glory among the heathen, his wonders among all people.

For the Lord is great, and greatly to be praised: he is to be feared above all gods.

For all the gods of the nations are idols: but the Lord made the heavens.

Honour and majesty are before him: strength and beauty are in his sanctuary.

Give unto the Lord, O ye kindreds of the people, give unto the Lord glory and strength.

Give unto the Lord the glory due unto his name: bring an offering, and come into his courts.

O worship the Lord in the beauty of holiness: fear before him, all the earth.

Say among the heathen that the Lord reigneth: the world also shall be established that it shall not be moved: he shall judge the people righteously.

283 Christat Foretold

Isaiah 9: 2-7; 7: 14

The people that walked in darkness have seen a great light:

They that dwell in the land of the shadow of death, upon them hath the light shined.

Thou hast multiplied the nation, and not increased the joy:

They joy before thee according to the joy in harvest, and as men rejoice when they divide the spoil.

For thou hast broken the yoke of his burden, and the staff of his shoulder, the rod of his oppressor, as in the day of Midian.

For every battle of the warrior is with confused noise, and garments rolled in blood; but this shall be with burning and fuel of fire.

For unto us a child is born, unto us a son is given: and the government shall be upon his shoulder:

And his name shall be called W o n d e r f u l , Counsellor, The mighty God, The everlasting Father, The Prince of Peace.

Of the increase of his government and peace there shall be no end, upon the throne of David, and upon his kingdom, to order it, and to establish it with judgment and with justice from henceforth even for ever.

The zeal of the Lord of hosts will perform this.

The Lord himself shall give you a sign;

Behold, a virgin shall conceive, and bear a son, and shall call his name Immanuel.

284 Christ Fulfilling

Luke 2: 7-16

And she brought forth her firstborn son, and wrapped him in swaddling clothes, and laid him in a manger; because there was no room for them in the inn.

And there were in the same country shepherds abiding in the field, keeping watch over their flock by night.

And, lo, the angel of the Lord came upon them, and the glory of the Lord shone round about them: and they were sore afraid.

And the angel said unto them, Fear not: for, behold, I bring you good tidings of great joy, which shall be to all people.

For unto you is born this day in the city of David a Saviour, which is Christ the Lord.

And this shall be a sign unto you; Ye shall find the babe wrapped in swaddling clothes, lying in a manger.

And suddenly there was with the angel a multitude of the heavenly host praising God, and saying,

Glory to God in the highest, and on earth peace, good will toward men.

And it came to pass, as the angels were gone away from them into heaven, the shepherds said one to another, Let us now go even unto Bethlehem, and see this thing which is come to pass.

And they came with haste, and found Mary, and Joseph, and the babe lying in a manger.

285 Christ Inviting

Matthew 11: 28-30; Isaiah 55: 1-3;
John 6: 37-38, 40

Come unto me, all ye that labour and are heavy laden, and I will give you rest.

Take my yoke upon you, and learn of me; for I am meek and lowly in heart:

And ye shall find rest unto your souls.

For my yoke is easy, and my burden is light.

Ho, every one that thirsteth, come ye to the waters, and he that hath no money; come ye, buy, and eat; yea, come, buy wine and milk without money and without price.

Wherefore do ye spend money for that which is not bread? and your labour for that which satisfieth not? hearken diligently unto me, and eat ye that which is good, and let your soul delight itself in fatness.

Incline your ear, and come unto me: hear, and your soul shall live; and I will make an everlasting covenant with you, even the sure mercies of David.

All that the Father giveth me shall come to me: and him that cometh to me I will in no wise cast out.

For I came down from heaven, not to do mine own will, but the will of him that sent me.

And this is the will of him that sent me, that every one which seeth the Son, and believeth on him, may have everlasting life: and I will raise him up at the last day.

286 Christ Saving

John 3: 14-21; 20: 31

And as Moses lifted up the serpent in the wilderness, even so must the Son of man be lifted up:

That whosoever believeth in him should not perish, but have eternal life.

For God so loved the world, that he gave his only begotten Son, that whosoever believeth in him should not perish, but have everlasting life.

For God sent not his Son into the world to condemn the world; but that the world through him might be saved.

He that believeth on him is not condemned: but he that believeth not is condemned already, because he hath not believed in the name of the only begotten Son of God.

And this is the condemnation, that light is come into the world, and men loved darkness rather than light, because their deeds were evil.

For every one that doeth evil hateth the light, neither cometh to the light, lest his deeds should be reproved.

But he that doeth truth cometh to the light, that his deeds may be made manifest, that they are wrought in God.

These are written, that ye might believe that Jesus is the Christ, the Son of God;

And that believing ye might have life through his name.

Matthew 5: 3-14, 16

Blessed are the poor in spirit: for theirs is the kingdom of heaven.

Blessed are they that mourn: for they shall be comforted.

Blessed are the meek: for they shall inherit the earth.

Blessed are they which do hunger and thirst after righteousness: for they shall be filled.

Blessed are the merciful: for they shall obtain mercy.

Blessed are the pure in heart for they shall see God.

Blessed are the peacemakers: for they shall be called the children of God.

Blessed are they which are persecuted for righteousness' sake: for theirs is the kingdom of heaven.

Blessed are ye, when men shall revile you, and persecute you, and shall say all manner of evil against you falsely, for my sake.

Rejoice, and be exceeding glad: for great is your reward in heaven: for so persecuted they the prophets which were before you.

Ye are the salt of the earth: but if the salt have lost his savour, wherewith shall it be salted? it is thenceforth good for nothing, but to be cast out, and to be trodden under foot of men.

Ye are the light of the world. A city that is set on an hill cannot be hid.

Let your light so shine before men, that they may see your good works, and glorify your Father which is in heaven.

Revelation 7: 9-15, 17

After this I beheld, and, lo, a great multitude, which no man could number, of all nations, and kindreds, and people, and tongues, stood before the throne, and before the Lamb, clothed with white robes, and palms in their hands;

And cried with a loud voice, saying, Salvation to our God which sitteth upon the throne, and unto the Lamb.

And all the angels stood round about the throne, and about the elders and the four beasts, and fell before the throne on their faces, and worshipped God,

Saying, Amen: Blessing, and glory, and wisdom, and thanksgiving, and honour, and power, and might, be unto our God for ever and ever. Amen.

And one of the elders answered, saying unto me, What are these which are arrayed in white robes? and whence came they?

And I said unto him, Sir, thou knowest. And he said to me, These are they which came out of great tribulation, and h a v e washed their robes, and made them white in the blood of the Lamb.

Therefore are they before the throne of God, and serve him day and night in his temple: and he that sitteth on the throne shall dwell among them.

For the Lamb which is in the midst of the throne shall feed them, and shall lead them unto living fountains of waters: and God shall wipe away all tears from their eyes

Now faith is the substance of things hoped for, the evidence of things not seen.

By faith Abel offered unto God a more excellent sacrifice than Cain, by which he obtained witness that he was righteous, God testifying of his gifts: and by it he being dead yet speaketh.

By faith Enoch was translated that he should not see death; and was not found, because God had translated him: for before his translation he had this testimony, that he pleased God.

But without faith it is impossible to please him: for he that cometh to God must believe that he is, and that he is a rewarder of them that diligently seek him.

By faith Noah, being warned of God of things not seen as yet, moved with fear, prepared an ark to the saving of his house; by the which he condemned the world, and became heir of the righteousness which is by faith.

By faith Abraham, when he was called to go out into a place which he should after receive for an inheritance, obeyed; and he went out, not knowing whither he went.

By faith he sojourned in the land of promise, as in a strange country, dwelling in tabernacles with Isaac and Jacob, the heirs with him of the same promise:

For he looked for a city which hath foundations, whose builder and maker is God.

Though I speak with the tongues of men and of angels, and have not charity, I am become as sounding brass, or a tinkling cymbal.

And though I have the gift of prophecy, and understand all mysteries, and all knowledge; and though I have all faith, so that I could remove mountains, and have not charity, I am nothing.

And though I bestow all my goods to feed the poor, and though I give my body to be burned, and have not charity, it profiteth me nothing.

Charity suffereth long, and is kind; charity envieth not; charity vaunteth not itself, is not puffed up,

Doth not behave itself unseemly, seeketh not her own, is not easily provoked, thinketh no evil;

Rejoiceth not in iniquity, but rejoiceth in the truth;

Beareth all things, believeth all things, hopeth all things, endureth all things.

Charity never faileth: b u t whether there be prophecies, they shall fail; whether there be tongues, they shall cease; whether there be knowledge, it shall vanish away.

For we know in part, and we prophesy in part. But when that which is perfect is come, then that which is in part shall be done away.

When I was a child, I spake as a child, I understood as a child, I thought as a child: but when I became a man, I put away childish things.

For now we see through a glass darkly; but then face to face: now I know in part; but then shall I know even as also I am known.

291 My Shepherd

Psalms 23; John 10: 11, 14-17

The Lord is my shepherd; I shall not want.

He maketh me to lie down in green pastures: he leadeth me beside the still waters.

He restoreth my soul: he leadeth me in the paths of righteousness for his name's sake.

Yea, though I walk through the valley of the shadow of death, I will fear no evil: for thou art with me; thy rod and thy staff they comfort me.

Thou preparest a table before me in the presence of mine enemies: thou anointest my head with oil; my cup runneth over.

Surely goodness and mercy shall follow me all the days of my life: and I will dwell in the house of the Lord for ever.

I am the good shepherd: the good shepherd giveth his life for the sheep. . . . I am the good shepherd, and know my sheep, and am known of mine.

As the Father knoweth me, even so know I the Father: and I lay down my life for the sheep.

And other sheep I have, which are not of this fold: them also I must bring, and they shall hear my voice; and there shall be one fold, and one shepherd.

Therefore doth my Father love me, because I lay down my life, that I might take it again.

292 My Healer

Luke 4: 38-40; 17: 12-17, 19

And he arose out of the synagogue, and entered into Simon's house.

And Simon's wife's mother was taken with a great fever; and they besought him for her.

And he stood over her, and rebuked the fever; and it left her: and immediately she arose and ministered unto them.

Now when the sun was setting, all they that had any sick with divers diseases brought them unto him;

And he laid his hands on every one of them, and healed them.

And as he entered into a certain village, there met him ten men that were lepers, which stood afar off:

And they lifted up their voices, and said, Jesus, Master, have mercy on us.

And when he saw them, he said unto them, Go shew yourselves unto the priests. And it came to pass, that, as they went, they were cleansed.

And one of them, when he saw that he was healed, turned back, and with a loud voice glorified God,

And fell down on his face at his feet, giving him thanks: and he was a Samaritan.

And Jesus answering said, Were there not ten cleansed? but where are the nine?

And he said unto him, Arise, go thy way: thy faith hath made thee whole.

293 My Light

Psalms 27: 1-11, 13-14

The Lord is my light and my salvation; whom shall I fear? the Lord is the strength of my life; of whom shall I be afraid?

When the wicked, even mine enemies and my foes, came upon me to eat up my flesh, they stumbled and fell.

Though an host should encamp against me, my heart shall not fear: though war should rise against me, in this will I be confident.

One thing have I desired of the Lord, that will I seek after;

That I may dwell in the house of the Lord all the days of my life, to behold the beauty of the Lord, and to enquire in his temple.

For in the time of trouble he shall hide me in his pavilion:

In the secret of his tabernacle shall he hide me; he shall set me up upon a rock.

And now shall mine head be lifted up above mine enemies round about me:

Therefore will I offer in his tabernacle sacrifices of joy; I will sing, yea, I will sing praises unto the Lord.

Hear, O Lord, when I cry with my voice: have mercy also upon me, and answer me.

When thou saidst, Seek ye my face; my heart said unto thee, Thy face, Lord, will I seek.

Hide not thy face far from me; put not thy servant away in anger: thou hast been my help; leave me not, neither forsake me, O God of my salvation.

When my father and my mother forsake me, then the Lord will take me up.

Teach me thy way, O Lord, and lead me in a plain path, because of mine enemies.

I had fainted, unless I had believed to see the goodness of the Lord in the land of the living.

Wait on the Lord: be of good courage, and he shall strengthen thine heart: wait I say, on the Lord.

294 My Help

Psalms 121

I will lift up mine eyes unto the hills, from whence cometh my help.

My help cometh from the Lord, which made heaven and earth.

He will not suffer thy foot to be moved: he that keepeth thee will not slumber.

Behold, he that keepeth Israel shall neither slumber nor sleep.

The Lord is thy keeper: the Lord is thy shade upon thy right hand.

The sun shall not smite thee by day, nor the moon by night.

The Lord shall preserve thee from all evil: he shall preserve thy soul.

The Lord shall preserve thy going out and thy coming in from this time forth, and even for evermore.

295 The Commandments

Exodus 20: 3-5a, 7-8, 12-17; ·*Matthew* 22: 36-39

Thou shalt have no other gods before me.

Thou shalt not make unto thee any graven image, or any likeness of any thing that is in heaven above, or that is in the earth beneath, or that is in the water under the earth: Thou shalt not bow down thyself to them, nor serve them:

Thou shalt not take the name of the Lord thy God in vain; for the Lord will not hold him guiltless that taketh his name in vain.

Remember the sabbath day, to keep it holy.

Honour thy father and thy mother: that thy days may be long upon the land which the Lord thy God giveth thee.

Thou shalt not kill.

Thou shalt not commit adultery.

Thou shalt not steal.

Thou shalt not bear false witness against thy neighbour.

Thou shalt not covet.

Master, which is the great commandment in the law?

Jesus said unto him, Thou shalt love the Lord thy God with all thy heart, and with all thy soul, and with all thy mind.

This is the first and great commandment.

And the second is like unto it, Thou shalt love thy neighbour as thyself.

296   Faithfulness

Matthew· 24: 45-47; *Luke* 16: 10-13; ·*Revelation* 2: 10b; *1 Corinthians* 15: 57-58

Who then is a faithful and wise servant, whom his lord hath made ruler over his household, to give them meat in due season?

Blessed is that servant, whom his lord when he cometh shall find so doing.

Verily I say unto you, That he shall make him ruler over all his goods.

He that is faithful in that which is least is faithful also in much: and he that is unjust in the least is unjust also in much.

If therefore ye have not been faithful in the unrighteous mammon, who will commit to your trust the true riches?

And if ye have not been faithful in that which is another man's, who shall give you that which is your own?

No servant can serve two masters: for either he will hate the one, and love the other; or else he will hold to the one, and despise the other. Ye cannot serve God and mammon.

Be thou faithful unto death, and I will give thee a crown of life.

Thanks be to God, which giveth us the victory through our Lord Jesus Christ.

Therefore, my beloved brethren, be ye stedfast, unmovable, always abounding in the work of the Lord, forasmuch as ye know that your labour is not in vain in the Lord.

297 Liberality

Psalms 41: 1-3; Mark 12: 41-44; II Corinthians 8: 1-5

Blessed is he that considereth the poor: the Lord will deliver him in time of trouble.

The Lord will preserve him, and keep him alive; and he shall be blessed upon the earth: and thou wilt not deliver him unto the will of his enemies.

The Lord will strengthen him upon the bed of languishing: thou wilt make all his bed in his sickness.

And Jesus sat over against the treasury, and beheld how the people cast money into the treasury: and many that were rich cast in much.

And there came a certain poor widow, and she threw in two mites, which make a farthing.

And he called unto him his disciples, and saith unto them, Verily I say unto you, That this poor widow hath cast more in, than all they which have cast into the treasury:

For all they did cast in of their abundance; but she of her want did cast in all that she had, even all her living.

Moreover, brethren, we do you to wit of the grace of God bestowed on the churches of Macedonia;

How that in a great trial of affliction the abundance of their joy and their deep poverty abounded unto the riches of their liberality.

For to their power, I bear record, yea, and beyond their power they were willing of themselves;

Praying us with much intreaty that we would receive the gift, and take upon us the fellowship of the ministering to the saints.

And this they did, not as we hoped, but first gave their own selves to the Lord, and unto us by the will of God.

298 Missions

Mark· 16: 15; Romans 10: 8-15

And he said unto them, Go ye into all the world, and preach the gospel to every creature.

But what saith it? The word is nigh thee, even in thy mouth, and in thy heart: that is, the word of faith, which we preach;

That if thou shalt confess with thy mouth the Lord Jesus, and shalt believe in thine heart that God hath raised him from the dead, thou shalt be saved.

For with the heart man believeth unto righteousness; and with the mouth confession is made unto salvation.

For the scripture saith, Whosoever believeth on him shall not be ashamed.

For there is no difference between the Jew and the Greek: for the same Lord over all is rich unto all that call upon him.

For whosoever shall call upon the name of the Lord shall be saved.

How then shall they call on him in whom they have not believed? and how shall they believe in him of whom they have not heard?

And how shall they hear without a preacher?

And how shall they preach, except they be sent?

Benedictions

The Lord bless thee and keep thee: The Lord make
his face shine upon thee, and be gracious unto thee:
the Lord lift up his countenance upon thee,
and give thee peace. Amen.
Numbers 6:24, 26

Now the God of peace, that brought again from the
dead our Lord Jesus Christ, that great Shepherd of the
sheep, through the blood of the everlasting covenant,
make you perfect in every good work to do his will,
working in you that which is wellpleasing in his sight,
through Jesus Christ; to whom be glory for ever
and ever. Amen.
Hebrews 13:20, 21

Now our Lord Jesus Christ himself, and God, even
our Father, which hath loved us, and hath given us
everlasting consolation and good hope through grace,
Comfort your hearts and stablish you in every
good word and work. Amen.
II Thessalonians 2:16, 17

Now unto him that is able to keep you from falling,
and to present you faultless before the presence of his
glory with exceeding joy, to the only wise God our Saviour,
be glory and majesty, dominion and power,
both now and ever. Amen.
Jude 24, 25

The grace of our Lord Jesus Christ be with your
spirit. Amen.
Philemon 25

COMPLETE TOPICAL INDEX

This Cross Index will assist in planning religious services. The appropriate song for any occasion, or for any subject can easily be selected.

TOPICAL INDEX

TOPICAL INDEX

TOPICAL INDEX

GENERAL INDEX

Titles in Caps & Small Caps -- First lines in lower case -- Chorus in Italics

GENERAL INDEX

GENERAL INDEX

GENERAL INDEX

GENERAL INDEX